TABLE OF CONTENTS

ACKNOWLEDGEMENTS

There are so many that I would like to recognize and thank.

Thank you my Lord and Savior Jesus Christ. As said in Philippians 4:13, "I can do all things through you, who strengthens me."

Thank you all who are named, remain unnamed, and some who may not even be mentioned in this book. I think about you often and am thankful for all you've taught me while I have watched you on your own journeys, and while you have helped shape and accompany me on mine. There are too many people to list here, but if you think I may be speaking of you, just know that I am, and I cherish our friendship.

Thank you Dad for being my first Hero in life. You suffer no more and I can't wait to see you again.

Thank you Mom for teaching me to be a fighter. You taught me through your actions.

Thank you Kane, Jayda and Harrison. The three of you are my heart and my biggest blessing. You are all so special in your own way. I pray you can understand your power, gifts and beauty. I release you into this dark world to brighten it with your own light, and I don't encourage, but demand you to attack life. Go own it.

Thank you Christina. You are brutally honest, and that is just scratching the surface of why I love you. You have opened my eyes, are my inspiration to achieve more, and are the backbone of our family. Without you, the life we have created and share would not be possible. You are my biggest supporter.

This book is for you.

PROLOGUE:

WAKE UP

This book may ruffle a few feathers. Good.

Welcome to the wake up call.

I speak from my heart. I've been chastised and debated over what I believe to be the key principles of mindset and success. Those that oppose me on one end say I am too "unrealistic" (you know, puppies and rainbows), while others tag me as too harsh (how could I think that way) and argue that I should preach empathy.

I absolutely understand that there are some out there who we deem less fortunate. There are so many of us who come from disadvantageous backgrounds and upbringings. That's exactly why I write these words. The very individuals who are in those positions need this message even more. Actually, we all do.

I'm speaking directly to you. It doesn't matter how important you are, how insignificant you may see yourself, what is or is not in your bank account or what title you do or do not have. Your age is irrelevant, and your past success or failure carries no merit here. Understand that I want to smash any victim mentality or scarcity mindset. Dominance is a mindset. You, I'm speaking to *you*, can capture this mindset. YOU can be dominant!

Listen, this book is pretty black and white. Reading these pages will either offend you, or inspire you. I hope it's the latter, but there really is no middle ground. If you are offended, that's not on me, it's you. I'm really just holding the mirror and calling it like I see it.

I feel many of the subjects I cover can be sensitive topics because deep down they will resonate with so many who either chose to identify, embrace and act - or - suppress, rationalize and dismiss.

I'm not afraid to write about how one person can post on social media that they started a business and receive 14 likes while someone else can post that they hate sitting in traffic and rack up 173 likes, 50 comments and two pms. The herd mentality, the "less than" attitude is garbage. It doesn't serve you, and you need to lose it.

I'm not comfortable with comfortable. I'm not okay with okay. I am here to fire it up and hopefully fire you up, too. You want more, you deserve more and you can have more. The purpose of this book is to help you visualize your greater purpose, inspire you to dream crazy big, propel you to attack your goals, and achieve your success - whatever that may look like for you.

Know that I have written this book with best intentions and I am delivering it with no fluff and real talk. Together we're gonna make this journey happen. Let's shake things up and get to where you want to be. Grab my hand, trust me and let's go!

RANT #1

GET UP

Get up! Get up, already. Sometimes we all need a hard kick in the rear to redirect how we think and what we do. So this is that kick. Get up!

You know better. You are better, and you know that too. We all get tired. We all get low. We all fall down. It's life. The unwritten rule is that you're just not allowed to stay tired, low or down.

I know. It's heavy. I wouldn't understand.

Any trials or hardships I've faced are waaaay different than what you have going on now. And that suffocating feeling of heaviness? I couldn't possibly know what it's like. Even if I did, maybe I'm just stronger than you. Right? Wrong, cupcake.

Check this out: If you can read or hear this, if you can *BREATHE* right now - yes, even with a machine that gives you assistance (because excuses aren't allowed) - you are still here. You have purpose. And you're blessed.

Not buying it? There are tons of souls who would trade their position with yours in a heartbeat, right now. And I'm taking the liberty of making that bold statement on behalf of so many of my friends and family who aren't here anymore. I'm sure they would gladly inherit your problem quickly for an opportunity. One more day. One more step. One more breath. One more chance.

So, here comes the tough love part. I'm not asking you what are you going to do with that extra day or chance. I'm saying to you how DARE you not do something with it!

Too many others are effected by your choices and actions, or your lack of choices and actions. So choose. Act.

You have energy. You have power. You have unique talents and gifts that no one else does - not like you do - and you know that to be true.

So, that low point? It ends here.

That tired feeling? Reenergize. Take a freakin' vitamin if you need to. You have much left to do.

Your heart was broken? That's okay. The person who puts it back together for you will make it that much better.

You fell down? Yep, it sucks. But it's life. We all do. But, now it's time. It's time to rise. Get up.

1

FIGHT FOR FAITH

*"Faith is taking the first step, even when you
don't see the whole staircase."*

\- Dr. Martin Luther King Jr.

Oh, I know it's hard. You may not know me yet, but you can believe me. I'm by your side - right here - in these daily trenches of life every, single day. I'm battling, just like you are. And just like you, I am scratching, crawling, striving for what can seem like that ever elusive struggle to win.

All those obstacles? Those punishing, relentless, heavy, daily obstacles? I know who they are, and they know me, too. They are my enemies. Unfortunately, I've spent so much time with some of them that we are on a first name basis.

Meet frustration.

I understand frustration. We grew up together. All too well, I recognize that blistering emotion that can bring you…well, me, to the brink of bitter rage and explosion. The burning tears. I can feel them. Nothing good ever comes from frustration. I teach my children "If you lose your cool, you lose." While I boil, it mocks and laughs at me. Frustration is humiliating and nasty.

Hopelessness.

I have experienced hopelessness. That sick, hollow feel of empty. The hopelessness of loss - whether that loss is in the form of an opportunity, a person, or even part of yourself can immediately shut you down. It is a bottomless pit that can swallow you whole. When hopelessness shows it's face, I groan internally, because I know (as always) it is going to leave my spirit feeling drained and depleted.

Defeat.

Regrettably, I know the lie named defeat all too well. We go way back. I also recognize the feeling of humiliation to the ego, the crushing blow to the self-esteem in knowing that I wasn't good enough. That awful embarrassment of thinking "Maybe next time" is debilitating. My disdain for defeat has always superseded my adulation for victory. I don't do hate much, but I loathe defeat.

Maybe my next enemy is one of yours also.

Fear.

Fear is very sly and can arrive uninvited and without warning. Anxiety. Worry. Not being able to sleep well.

Fear of the future. Fear of being afraid. It's paralyzing. Fear and I have spent time together on numerous occasions. Whenever we do, I question myself why I've allowed it. As convincing as it is, fear is a liar and I should know better.

Every single one of these daily challenges or "speed bumps" (as I refer to them) and all those other ones that I fail to mention - you know - the ones you and I both struggle with, are something that you, and I, and every other person on the planet do and actually *must* experience. You don't need me to tell you what you already know, but maybe you need me to simply remind you. All these speed bumps are part of the journey. This collaborative explosion of everything we deal with shapes the body of work of the person we become.

Sadly, these emotional speed bumps of despair that we do not desire to hit are a must. It's not a question of if. It's a question of when, and at some point, we all will encounter them. However, there is good news.

We don't have to stay with them.

We can leave them behind. *You* can leave them behind. Really. And you can leave them behind anytime you want. It's a choice, and you can choose.

You see, like I said, I know how hard it is - this day-to-day cycle. I know how punishing, how relentless, heavy, draining, and how crippling it can be.

But that was learned.

So, fortunately for me (and hopefully anyone who is reading or listening to this), I've learned a few other things too.

See, I am by your side - right here - in these daily trenches of life every single day, battling just like you are. I am scratching, crawling, striving for what can seem like that ever elusive struggle to win.

And I've found some weapons along the way. These weapons are my friends. When they show up, they bring a smile to my face. I take great care of them, and they take great care of me. When we get together, we become unstoppable. These weapons destroy the speed bumps. Maybe these weapons - my friends - are friends of yours, too.

Allow me to introduce...Gratitude.

Things can always be better. We can always achieve more, and we will always aspire to go higher. We as human beings are insatiable, and we can't help that. I don't even necessarily feel that this is a bad thing. But there is something about human perspective of where you are at, where you came from, and *appreciating* it. Craving abundance for all the right reasons is admirable, but having an attitude of gratefulness is paramount. Look at it this way, if you are able to read this right now, you are truly blessed. Everyday is Thanksgiving.

Patience.

We took a long time to finally connect, that is, myself and patience. When we do get together, there is this calming clarity. There is an indescribable power of knowing that my friend patience has total superiority over that speed bump we call frustration. Patience presents this lucid contentment to understand that moments, situations, people, whatever - are the way they are, and it probably has nothing to do with you. No frustration required. Patience is an elusive friend with quiet strength, but once you've made that connection, one of your best friends it will be.

Relentlessness is one of my favorites.

We hang out often. What a powerful weapon. It's that rebellious friend that brings you to life! Relentlessness is like money. It's neither good or bad, it's all in how you choose to use it. If money is used to purchase illegal drugs for kids on a playground, it's bad. If money is used to feed and shelter the homeless, it's good.

Being relentless can also be taken as pigheaded or stubborn. I choose to identify it as a positive. You may recognize this in the form of dedication, perseverance, resolve, tenacity or spirit. Relentless can handle both speed bumps of defeat and hopelessness simultaneously. Relentlessness is dominant, it is unapologetic, and I am absolutely thrilled to call it my friend.

There are so many more "weapons" or friends that I've made along the way. They way outnumber my enemies. Without this next one though, none of the others can even exist. As a matter of fact, I view this next weapon of mine as a little more than a friend. When this one shows up, it's as if Daddy came home. Meet the most powerful tool in any arsenal. Meet my best friend.

Meet faith.

Faith is power, grace, beauty - the foundation and platform for every other positive attribute to stand on. You must have it. You must find it. It is CRUCIAL for your existence. Faith is an interesting friend to have. You can't see it, you can't touch it, and it's so hard to explain to someone who doesn't have it.

You may have heard before that faith - or belief - has a sound. You have to believe. Believe that things will get better. Believe that *you* will get better. Believe that you can, will and do make a difference.

See, belief (or faith) is an idea. Ideas become words. Words become things. Things become impactful. Faith is impactful! Anything that we know of, what you are sitting on right now (we sit too much), the attire that you are wearing, the book or device pumping this audio so you can see, read or hear this at this very moment is impactful. They are things. At one time, they were words. In their infancy, they were ideas. Those ideas were spawned with the belief - and faith - that they could become real. Faith is real.

Faith is supreme.

There is one caveat, however. I believe that if you don't protect what you have it will be taken away. Read that again.

If you don't protect what you have, it will be taken away.

If not guarded, faith can be taken away.

Those nasty enemies of mine, those same enemies of yours - remember them? Together those speed bumps of fear, frustration, hopelessness, and defeat can extinguish faith. That is if you let them.

If your bond with faith is broken, it is hard to reclaim. That's why you need to protect it, so it can't be taken away!

Look, the day-to-day can be ugly. Like it or not, choose to recognize and accept it or pretend otherwise - everyday is a battle. Fact. We battle circumstances, we battle principalities, and we constantly wrestle with ourselves. Everyday is a fight. Everyday we need faith.

We've walked alone before. Today is different. Today we take our first steps together, you and I. Today we protect what we have, and today we choose to fight for faith. Turn the page, read on, and keep fighting!

RANT #2

___

YOUR EXCUSES SUCK

They just do.

Excuses allow us the opportunity and convenience to have this comfortable, little safety net of failure. It lets us justify failure without remorse.

"Maybe I didn't achieve this time around, but it's alright. It only makes sense that I didn't hit my goal because _____ (Fill in the blank with your random excuse)."

Weak.

Everyone - yes, e-v-e-r-y-o-n-e from the most novice or insignificant, to the greatest of the great all have problems now and again. Roadblocks, potholes, speed bumps, closed bridges, flat tires and detours (not to mention all that traffic) can be found on the road to accomplishment.

In addition, most people are filled with fear. Fear of failure. Fear of success. Fear of what people will say. Fear of what people will think. Fear of the unknown. Fear of fake scenarios conjured up in their own minds. Fear of public speaking. Fear of dying. Some people are actually fearful of the idea of fear! It's fascinating.

The fact of the matter is that usually the fearful feeling is worse than whatever we are afraid of in the first place. What is the worst thing that could actually happen to you if you were to stand in front of 100 people with a microphone? Will angry villagers attack you with torches and pitchforks? No. Fear is a liar.

Fear is usually kept on the back burner - until the first sign of resistance happens. Oh, and resistance *will* happen. Do you think the Universe will just give you what you want - *and* let you keep it without proving yourself worthy? There is no entitlement or easy road to success.

Some people call it "Murphy's Law," I say spiritual warfare. Regardless, resistance happens, and now the drama that comes with it. What happens next? Permission. We tend to give ourselves permission to stand on that fear and allow it to rear it's ugly head in the form of an excuse.

Excuses are toxic. They can poison our minds and potentially damage our spirit with the lies we tell ourselves. We all have random excuses ready in place so we don't have to push ourselves and feel that fear of failure if we fall short. Some may say that they didn't want to earn the company trip to Mexico - because they don't like to travel. Some may not go for that company car they can earn - because they don't like the color the company is offering it in. I've actually heard these. We hear all kinds.

"I was going to apply for that position, but I'm sure there are applicants who are more qualified than me. I'll polish up and try next time."

"Man I was so ready to nail that audition, but traffic was jammed up and I couldn't get there in time. There was nothing I could do."

"I was sooo going to get that varsity position on the team, but I was sick for a few days and not 100 percent. Plus, that other kid's uncle is the coach anyway so even if I did get it, I'm sure he'd be given my spot at some point."

Underqualified? Late? Sick? Excuses. They're all garbage. Smash excuses.

Late. Sick. Do you know who is sick? Me - when I hear excuses. Do you know who else was sick?

Walter Payton.

Who? He is only one of the greatest Super Bowl Champion, NFL Hall Of Fame running backs of all time. In 1977 Payton, or "Sweetness" as he was know by, set an NFL rushing record. In 40 carries, he rumbled for 275 yards. 275 yards! Those are video game numbers, but that's not the incredible part.

He did it with the flu.

The day before kickoff he started having "hot and cold flashes" and feeling "weak." Despite this, he didn't ask to sit. He didn't request to not dress at game time, or be pulled out, or even take a breather. He broke records - with the flu. He smashed excuses.

I believe you can smash excuses, too. How? By having zero tolerance. No excuses allowed. Having a no-matter-what mindset.

I've conversed with and interviewed hundreds of successful people who are present or former pro athletes, military heroes, best selling authors, executive national vice presidents of companies, and even human beings who have fought and defeated cancer. Regardless of background or journey, all of these amazing individuals posses similar traits. One consistent trait is a "no matter what" mindset. They possess that attitude before they even begin their journey.

Using the mental muscle for busting the ability to rationalize will get stronger the more you use it. It's just like any muscle you strengthen when you work it in a gym. The difference is the gym is your mind, and the gym is always open.

Excuses do suck. And if you continue to foster and accept them, you'll suck too. I'm not trying to be witty, I'm being direct. And I don't care if your ego gets bruised, I care that you identify the trash and take it out.

Most people will have an out, they'll have that safety net. Humanity will justify, rationalize and reason away. Few will make the decision (and yes, it is as easy as deciding) to not accept excuses. The truth is the majority of the population will fail - because - of their excuses. Be in the minority. Be different. No excuses.

2

SUCCESS, FAILURE AND WHAT WE TELL OURSELVES

*"Whether you think you can,
or think you can't, you're right."*

- Henry Ford

I have a friend. Believe it or not, I actually have a few, but in this chapter I'm speaking of this one friend in particular.

We've know each other for years, our families hang together on special occasions, etc. The comical part is that we couldn't be any more opposite. He's "Yin" and I'm "Yang" or maybe vice-versa. I'm a soldier for Christ, and he's the devil's advocate. I'm the guy wearing the rose colored glasses, and he's the fact-bearing realist.

Debating on certain subjects from religion to politics to really intense topics, such as what player has more value for your fantasy football squad is pretty much the norm.

I'm sure when he reads this chapter, we'll debate this too. I must say we always respect each other enough to listen to the other, it's sometimes civil at best, and when all is said and done we always remain friends.

On a side note (if I may), isn't it refreshing in this day and age where everyone has an opinion and seems to offend, and be offended by every little thing, that we can actually have a *friend* who we can disagree with, and at the end of the day still remain friends? More of that, please. Hashtag, tolerance. It's alright if everyone doesn't think exactly the way I think, as long as it stays respectful.

Anyhow, like I was saying before I distracted myself… debating is the norm. And as I stated we always remain friends, but sometimes the conversation can get heated. Like the other day.

We were yelling and screaming at one another - via text message, of course (Another norm). You know. All words are in caps lock and you type really, really hard. The topic of this ferocious debate was the topic of success. I'll spare you all the brutal details, but the focus came down specifically to one of his kids.

"Andy is never going to make the NBA, he knows it, and we're alright with it. He's happy. What's wrong with that?"

My response was something to the effect of "I never said there was anything wrong with not making the NBA. And I'm happy he's happy. And you are absolutely right."

There was that awkward 30-second interval of no reply, and then here they come - the response bubbles hovering on his side of the text. Nevermind addressing "I'm happy he's happy," or "I never said there was anything wrong with not making the NBA." He responded with:

"What do you mean I'm right?"

Here we go. I was tempted to amuse myself and torture him with meaningless emojis. Instead, I used self restraint, and sent him my short but direct response.

"You're right. He's never going to make the NBA. It has nothing to do with talent. It has everything to do with the fact that you TOLD him he's never going to make the NBA." Angry emoji.

Why do we do this? Why do we put limitations on others and more importantly ourselves? So many of us play small, aim low, miss the opportunity and then have the regret of the "could of 's," "should of 's" and "would of 's." So unfortunate. If you take out the head, the body will fall. Many times we willingly and unknowingly take out our own head.

My friend's son (yes, we are still friends) is a really tremendous athlete. At this pace however, he will probably never make the NBA. Let's be honest. Most people won't. That is an elite fraternity that has a mixture of blood, sweat, tears, talent, skill and hard work. There is a mammoth difference between the players on any professional team, and their fans who cheer for them.

But let's go there.

TIME TO GO PRO

"Don't wish it were easier, wish you were better."
- Jim Rohn

Let's say "Andy" (not his actual name) woke up every morning 2-1/2 hours before school starts. Ouch, right? But we said the NBA. The NB freaking A. We didn't say the local township league. That means he may have to go to bed possibly 2 hours earlier! 8-9 o'clock? For a High School kid? Unheard of!

As I was saying, Andy wakes up 2-1/2 hours before the bell rings. That gives an hour to eat, shower and prep, 30 minutes or so of travel time, and one full hour of practice. Free throws. Every. Single. Day. So what does that look like?

Monday - free throws. Tuesday - free throws. Wednesday (it's cold out) - free throws. Thursday (his shoulder is sore) - but, free throws. Friday (he's feeling a cold coming on but remember, Kurt Angle won the 1996 Olympic Gold Medal while wrestling with a broken freaking neck) life is tough, wear a cup. Free throws.

Let's say this regiment is repeated for a solid year. I don't think Andy *could* miss a free throw if he tried. Oh

- something else that would be helpful would be a dietician for these crucial years of growth. A personal trainer and speed coach would be imperative during the off-season (typically 9 months) as well as more conditioning and free throws. Free throws in addition to the morning session continue in the gym. Everyday. After practice. Last one to leave. Outwork everybody.

Sound hard? Absolutely! But we said the NBA, remember? If you *want* what successful people have, you need to *do* what successful people do - and sometimes more. I guarantee most peers in the high school basketball program in his school, probably his county - maybe his state - will not work that hard. Some will work hard, but not *that* hard. Most won't work at all - especially in the off-season when it's distraction central. That's when it's baseball season, time for the beach, or football is starting again.

Most already don't have the belief - or lack thereof - that they can make it to the Big League, so they won't even try. But Andy will.

How will that look (if in a course of a lifetime what seems to be a blip on the radar) if Andy wasn't gaming with his buddies online every night? What if he put down the countless wasted minutes and hours of goofy apps and social distractions like Snapchat? What if he put girls on hold for now. Seriously? Yeah. Seriously. Trust me -

when Andy goes pro, having a social life with the ladies will not be an issue for him. What would start to happen if while they all partied, he worked on him?

How about in addition to team practice, personal daily practice (those darn free throws), conditioning, and weight training along with the proper diet, he incorporates a training program for high school ballers. Those programs are available out there. He would gain such a competitive edge and get to work with the top players from a wide area in his peer group. You know. Iron sharpens iron. Or maybe he is the top player there, and his confidence grows as he sees the fruit of his labor. That's kind of important.

Let's add in some film. Say he watches film like a beast and becomes a true student of the game. He could pick his favorite players and study their game. He could add some of their weapons in his arsenal with of course, relentless practice. He could implement strategies and movements that would give him the advantage over any opponents who do not watch film, don't study, and aren't students of the game.

Now we've got something. Maybe we just went from Andy "never making the NBA" to actually having a legit shot.

I work with kids, schools, and sports teams all the time regarding mindset and attitude. It can be tricky because

I see all ends of the spectrum ranging from low self-confidence and no vision to the elitist attitude. I often see too much entitlement.

How I balance it all when working with these groups of kids, is by stripping it all down and bringing everyone back to the starting line.

I'm pretty direct in letting them all know that not every kid in the locker room will make the NBA. Not everyone in the training facility is the next heavyweight world champion. And everyone in the assembly will not be an Oscar winning actress, Youtube sensation or future president. Then I encourage them to look around, to look at themselves. Closely. Because some might.

So how does that work? Are two babies born, same height, same weight, same gender and God just proclaims that one will be triumphant and the other one won't? For the sake of addressing all of my debating realist friends, obviously I acknowledge that some are born more talented than others. That's not what we're talking about here. You've seen the t-shirt. "Hard work beats talent when talent doesn't work hard."

In our example here, Andy is a walking sweat stain. He is already good, but he's taking steps to become great with a crazy, sick work ethic! He's going to a place where he trains himself to become comfortable with being uncomfortable. I'm not trying to be cliche guy, I'm telling you that the relentless, hungry mindset isn't just what gets you to the top, it's what keeps you at the top. If you don't believe me, ask anyone at the top.

LAZY

"The world is full of willing people; some willing to work, the rest willing to let them."

- Robert Frost

We fail. Duh. Waiter, a table for Captain Obvious, please. Look, let's be honest. We all fall from time to time, but I think the more important factor to address is that *most* people are not good at what they do, and most people don't want to work.

Have you ever been in need of a contractor and they show up? On time? Have you ever been in need of a contractor and they not only show up on time, but they actually come back to finish the work? When they are supposed to? Wait. They cleaned up, too? Amazing! Holy mackerel, high five and hallelujah. We're gonna tell our friends, blow them up on social media and put them over big time on Yelp! Right?

The sobering reality is, maybe they're just plain good. All they did was what they were *supposed* to do. They should show up. On time. They need to come back to finish the work. They shouldn't try to rip you off. They didn't go above and beyond and blow you away with greatness. They just did the work.

But - they didn't "no show," they didn't charge you and arm an a leg, they didn't do shoddy work and they didn't leave their disgusting cigarette butts in your driveway like the deadbeats that did last time, right? These guys must be great! Either that, or our standards have lowered because of the low level of service we've been giving and receiving. I'm not burying contractors, I'm just using them as my example. But if anyone has a good one - send them my way!

The truth? Most people don't do what they say they are going to do. They don't show up, they don't respond, they don't get it done - whatever "it" is. That actually takes effort. So put in the effort, because that makes a world of difference.

There is a tremendous failure rate across the board in every industry. I believe this is in part because many want to wear that team jacket, but don't want to go to team practice. Realtors, network marketers, the grocery bagger at the supermarket, the singer…not everyone turns out to be a rockstar in their chosen field. But some do. Andy for example, has a chance to make it to the NBA. He's putting in the work. The kid is in overdrive! He's gone far and beyond 98 percent of his peer group with effort. But is that enough? Before we call his number on draft day, we're not there just yet. He could use a few more ingredients for his recipe of success. Let's explore them.

TENACITY

*"Never interrupt someone who is doing
what you said couldn't be done."*
- Amelia Earhart

In the summer of 1987, I reported to high school football camp as a sophomore. Unbeknownst to me, I was poised to be the starting left offensive guard for varsity. Offensive lineman are usually the bruisers. These are the guys who are the biggest, hardest hitting guys on the team. I weighed 135 pounds. That was up five pounds from freshman year. Insert cringe here. For any non football fans reading, this basically meant my job description was to square up head-to-head (literally) against teens sometimes two years older than me, and while being outweighed by potentially 100 pounds, have the assignment of physically outmuscling them for hours.

I overheard one coach say "That Hayford kid is tenacious."

I thought to myself "Great! What does that mean?"

It was violent. It was grueling. I loved it.

You have to love it, whatever "it" is. You have to want it. It is going to get ugly. You are going to be tired. That tedious five-day-a-week ritual that Andy is performing gets old. You won't "feel" like doing it. It's exhausting. Obstacles are coming. Brace for them. Then blow through them. Or fail.

I know. This is beyond tough love, this is just harsh. Here's the deal - this part is for people who are ON PURPOSE. This part is for the ones who keep showing up when that good feeling is gone and everyone else quits. This is for the kid who is hardwired to think he "isn't going to make the NBA." I'm not an electrician, but let the rewiring of the mental hardwiring begin.

WE FAIL

"Failure defeats losers but inspires winners."
- Robert Kiyosaki

So, we fail. I said it. We all do. But, it truly is about those who do not quit.

There is an old saying: When a child is learning to walk and falls down 50 times, he doesn't think to himself "Maybe this isn't for me." He keeps trying until he gets it right.

The greatest of the great, the biggest household names of our lifetime - no - in HISTORY have all failed. As a matter of fact, the bigger they failed and the harder they rebounded with that relentless tenacity - especially in the face of ugly - the more they are celebrated. Just look at this list of world renown, planet changing "failures."

Oprah Winfrey was fired as a news anchor from prime time news. She was told she "wasn't fit for TV." Oprah? Not fit for TV? I'm not quite sure how the landscape of talk show TV would have been without Oprah.

Walt Disney was fired from his newspaper gig because he was "lacking imagination" and had "no original ideas." Seriously? The guy created a culture riding on the back of a pretend mouse. Here's imagination. Imagine if he quit. Where the heck would we go on vacation?

Ludwig Van Beethoven is quoted with saying "Music should strike fire from the heart of man, and bring tears from the eyes of woman." Teachers proclaimed he was "hopeless at composing." Beethoven. Hopeless at composing. Some of the most classical of classic masterpiece symphonies have been composed by LVB, and then he went deaf. Tragic. Oh wait. He continued composing. Tenacious.

Pull out a $5 bill. I know. You don't carry cash. But if you did, you would see the 16th President Of The United States Of America. Abraham Lincoln was president during the Civil War and ended slavery. Prior to those accomplishments his fiance died, multiple businesses of his collapsed, and he was defeated in 8 elections. Then he had a nervous breakdown. You think? Now he's on a $5 bill. But you don't have one because everything is automated. I digress.

My all time favorite "famous failure" is the greatest music group of all time. No, it's not U2. It's not Van Halen. It's not Led Zeppelin, and it's definitely not 98 Degrees. What? Anyway - it's The Beatles.

Am I sure this is the greatest group of all time? People, I've been a DJ for almost 20 years and a music enthusiast my entire life. This is the only group in the history of history to have twenty charted number-one hits where each and every member of the band (John Lennon, Paul McCartney, George Harrison, Ringo Starr) have separately sung lead vocals on at least one of those charted, number one hits. This has never been done before or since. When the group disbanded in 1970, all four members went on to not only have their own successful solo careers, tours and record sales, but their own number one hits. Yes, this is even including the drummer, Ringo Starr. Again, we've never seen that before, and perhaps we'll never see it again. Greatest group of all time. Incredible.

What's even more incredible is that Decca Records rejected them. Upon refusing to sign them, a representative from the recording studio was quoted as saying "We don't like their sound - they have no future in show business." Oops. Decca quickly made moves to redeem themselves and signed the Rolling Stones. Score! You can't always get what you want, but if you try sometimes, you get what you need.

I could write an entire separate book continuing on the focus of "famous failures." This list would be littered with superstars like Michael Jordan, Albert Einstein, Steve Jobs, Marilyn Monroe, Colonel Sanders, and Sir Isaac Newton just to name a few.

All of these now world-wide celebrated household names have failed. Miserably. Several times. They've all been told to quit and find another occupation because they weren't wanted and they weren't good enough. But they wanted it, and they didn't listen. They never stopped until they made their breakthrough. Sometimes the biggest breakthroughs happen once you decide to reject rejection. That is tenacity.

If you are reading this book at nighttime and can see the print because of lighting, you can thank New Jersey's own Thomas Edison. Edison created the lightbulb and was known as "America's Greatest Inventor." His most famous quote gives astounding perspective. "I haven't failed, I've just found 10,000 ways that won't work." Wow. Welcome to the granddaddy of tenacity.

Keep shooting those free throws, Andy. You have hope. But before you step onto the court for that NBA tryout, there's one more thing you need...

PMA

What? I thought we were talking about the NBA. Quiet! *Smack*

PMA is positive mental attitude.

Oh look! Here come the skeptics, realists and debunkers running back up to the stage for a chance to scoff and disregard this as fairy dust, rainbows and unicorns. We've been expecting you. Please, take a seat.

What's that? You say having a positive mental attitude or PMA is BS? Dude, it's scientific.

Dr. Shad Helmstetter has authored dozens of books over a handful of decades such as "What To Say When You Talk To Yourself," "The Gift," and "The Power Of Neuroplasticity." The power of what? Exactly. Listen and learn you realistic, skeptical haters.

I was able to sit down and interview Helmstetter who is the creator of the "Self Talk Institute." Here are some excerpts from the interview showcasing what he had to say regarding the legitimate scientific explanation on the power of positivity and what we tell ourselves.

"Self talk is something we all do. But as I write about it, self talk is a way of literally redefining your path, redefining your actions, redefining your attitudes all based on what you say when you talk to yourself."

He continued with, "What I have discovered was (from the field of neuroscience) that our thoughts actually wire our brain. We used to be taught that the brain stops growing. That we only get so many neurons when you're young, and the brain stops growing, and then that's it for the rest of our lives. Then we lose a lot of those neurons, and we're out of luck."

"Well," Helmstetter said "It wasn't true at all. It was just because science yet hadn't found a way to look into the brain and scan it. Now we can do that, and what we've learned is that *our brain continues to grow and change throughout our entire lives.*"

When Dr. Shad revealed this data, I was stunned. You mean a 90-year-old with a healthy brain can continue to learn and grow? You mean you **can** teach an old dog new tricks? Myth busted. But he didn't stop there. Next came the critical part.

"The most important factor in things that change our brain is actually our thoughts. Repeated thoughts, repeated words, repeated messages actually rewire the brain... that means it isn't up to them...or our past. It doesn't make any difference where you've been...it's what you do now with what you've got, and the brain is *waiting* to be wired, and rewired, and rewired. We get to do that with our thoughts."

Hold up. Did he just insinuate that WE have the power over OURSELVES? We can actually *create* the type of person we want to be with a positive mental attitude and changing how we talk to ourselves with repetition? I believe he did.

THAT is neuroplasticity. Simply put, neuroplasticity is how the brain is hardwired and how you can upload any message you want and make it TRUE in that untapped resource, that magnificent computer, your brain.

I'm going to ask you a question.

I want your answer to be impulsive without much thought. Blurt out the first name that pops into that mental microchip of yours. Ready?

Who is the greatest boxer of all time?

No scrolling, looking down or changing your mind. Tell me, who did you automatically think of?

Muhammad Ali, right?

Most readers will answer yes to this. Ali was not only the 3 time Heavyweight Champion Of The World and renown activist, but he is one of the most significant and famed figures (in and outside of sports) of all time. But was he *really* the greatest?

Boxing enthusiasts may debate this claim. What about Joe Lewis? Mike Tyson? Does Floyd "Money" Mayweather, Jack Dempsey or Sugar Ray Robinson come to mind? They made a movie about Jake LaMotta too, you know. Box office smash "Raging Bull" won 24 out of 26 award nominations including the Oscar and Golden Globes. That's not an accident. Have you ever "knocked the fat outta food" with the Muhammad Ali Grill? Nope. Me neither. But I have several times on the George Foreman Grill! I mean Sugar Ray Robinson fought in two different weight classes and came close to *quadrupling* Ali's win record.

But Muhammad Ali popped into your mind. With over a century of all-time greats that can be rattled off, you immediately thought of Ali as the greatest. Why?

Because he said he was.

And he told us over and over and over again. He believed it. We believed it. Media fed it. Now it's folklore. He's the greatest.

I asked Helmstetter if he thought Ali used the power of positive self talk, or neuroplasticity. His answer was telling.

"Yes, he did. A lot of athletes did. As a matter of fact, that's where we first saw self talk in use - sports and athletics."

He added "At the time years ago when they first started using it, they really didn't understand how the process worked, but they knew the results. And the results were the people who BELIEVED they could do it...can literally talk to themselves in a way that gave them a picture in their minds of themselves accomplishing their goal. Those athletes tended to do better. *They would win.*"

The doctor is telling me that what Ali did, what athletes do, and simply put, anyone can literally talk themselves into winning.

"Scientific studies have been done on exactly that, and that's what happens."

Helmstetter went on to say that athletes who consistently practice positive self talk prior to an event (especially over lengthier periods of time prior to an event) can increase their endurance up to 18 percent. 18 percent? Mind blown.

He continued with encouraging parents to teach children, especially little children that as soon as they start to learn to talk during infancy all the way up to adulthood that positive self talk is critical. Critical. What you say to your children actually types a message into their brain.

I use the analogy of a blank CD. As a parent, coach, teacher, speaker, especially with children, you get to burn whatever message you want onto that compact disk and then it's there. Take caution what message you are programming. It can quickly shift from "I'll never make the NBA" to "I am an NBA Player" to "I am the greatest."

In my opinion Muhammad Ali was a walking fortune cookie for positive mental attitude. My opinion, my book. If you disagree, I encourage you to write your own.

For me, Ali had some of the finest quotes from anyone in pop culture. I'm not talking about "float like a butterfly, sting like a bee." I'm speaking of "I hated every minute of training, but I said...Don't quit. Suffer now and live the rest of your life as a champion," or "Don't count the days, make the days count." Ali was definitely the greatest - especially when it came to PMA.

But enough about Ali and back to Andy. I don't know if the young lad will ever make the NBA or not, and if not, I can't answer if he's fine with it. I do know this - if he does want to make it to that high level of competition, literally the best in the world, it's not overnight, and it's definitely not probable.

It is, however, possible. And only Andy is in control of what he is willing or not willing to do - how far he is willing to go to make that dream come true.

Don't ever let anyone ever tell you that you can't or you won't be able to achieve something. If you want the success, whether it's in the NBA, that job promotion, or any high level of achievement - you better be ready to work. You better be ready to outwork any level you've ever performed at before and commit to going all in.

Once that's in check, feed that most powerful asset - your mind. What you tell yourself - how you *currently* view yourself makes all the difference in the world.

If Andy walks, talks, acts, thinks, BECOMES an NBA player in his mind, we may just be seeing him smash a backboard one day. It's happened for others, why not him? Dream big.

And as far as Andy's outcome, I hope he decides to go for it, and I hope he makes it. If and when he does, I'll be the first in line to snatch up two of his jerseys. One for me, and one for his Dad.

RANT #3

FOCUS

Dr. Tom Barrett has authored many books such as "Dare To Dream And Work To Win," "Easy Street," and "Success Happens" just to name a few. There is one particular chapter where within the opening paragraphs he wrote the word "Focus" at least a million times. I'm obviously exaggerating but it went something to the tune of "Focus. It's how the tortoise beats the hare. Focus. It's etc, etc, etc. Focus..."

On and on and on and on. It was actually borderline obnoxious, but I think that was the point. Midway through the paragraph I actually started drifting off to somewhere else before I caught myself. He could have added "Focus. It's how Marc reads a book. Focus..."

People, we live right in the heart of Distractionville. I don't know who you are, where you live, or what you do, but I guarantee your cell phone is within arms reach. Solitare, Youtube, Snapchat, text messages, Facebook, email, software updates, Instagram, sports updates, breaking news...it's so easy to get nowhere fast these days. Have you ever just sat there muddling around with your phone and an hour later you wonder where the time went? Of course you have! And that thing - the thing you were going to get to? Well, that can just wait until tomorrow now, can't it?

We are set up to fail. The starting line of the race has us running uphill from the very bottom before the gun even fires. It gets worse and worse every year. Acceleration of technology has so many advantages, but not if we use it to fall down the rabbit hole of distractions.

There is such an overall lack of ambition and drive, too. Most people don't want to show up, or put in the effort when they do. That's not just these days, that's always. That is exactly why focus is essential to anything that will breed success.

Not always, but generally the ones who focus are the ones who win. Give yourself a chance. Phone away. Scheduled time. On purpose. Focus. Focus. Focus. Focus.

3

SELF STARTING

"Make it happen. Shock everyone."

- Unknown

It is imperative to self start. Understand this. It is one of the MOST important attributes you need to have in your arsenal if you are looking to be successful in any format. This is absolutely critical.

If you can train yourself to be a self starter, then 50 percent of the battle is won. And you can train yourself.

Personally speaking, I have come full circle with this. I went from not even being aware of the self starting concept to being pretty bad at it. From there, I went from bad to good, good to great, and now training others on how and why this is absolutely necessary.

Again, just attempting to be clear on this - I'm not referring to some cheerleading-type of encouragement for yourself that may come and go in waves. This isn't about psyching yourself up with a good feeling that will be fleeting, or gearing up for another potentially failing New Year Resolution.

This is about you navigating yourself through a noisy world that is littered with constant distractions ranging from heavy responsibilities to self indulging creature comforts and still being able to have the discipline to focus and show up on PURPOSE. On purpose is critical.

This is an art, and as the world gets busier and faster, the art is dying. So let's step into art class together.

SLEEP WALKING VS PROACTIVE

"The best way to predict the future is to create it."
- Peter Drucker

Please indulge me for the next few paragraphs while I absolutely brag about my previous monumental flaws. Yep, I'm going to tell you about how great I was at screwing up.

For a good portion of my life, self starting was not anywhere near being close on my radar. I did what so many do today, only I did it better. I was a world-class sleep walker. Most people you and I know sleep walk. They sleep walk through their entire lives. They wait for permission. They're looking for direction. They're told what to do. They obey. They're told what they're worth. They accept. They're okay with all of it.

I'm not suggesting anarchy here, I'm simply saying most people will go with the flow. We've been taught that it's been good to go with the flow. You know, roll with it. We've been taught wrong. It's a lie.

Calling an audible as life throws you a curve ball is different. Improvising when everything doesn't go as planned is another story.

Unless you are a US Marine where you are taught to "Improvise, adapt and overcome," or you are onstage performing as a musician in a jam band, I believe "going with the flow" is not only an attitude that will do you no favors, I believe it is dangerous. It falls right in line with that comfortable mindset. Comfortable doesn't grow, comfortable doesn't achieve, and comfortable never wins.

Like I said, I was an upper echelon, go with the flow sleep walker. You could put me in most situations and usually I would handle myself and come out not so much unscathed, but pretty decent.

Did you notice that? I said you could *put* me in most situations. Do you wait to be "put" in situations? Do you wait for permission? Direction? I sure did. It didn't serve me, and it definitely prevented me 100 percent from serving others. You cannot save other swimmers while you are drowning. Lose the anchor.

When sleep walking, I would be fantastic at reacting. I would almost always be reactive. It was far and between with the times when I would be proactive. That's what the pros do. They act. First. Purposely.

There is a night-and-day difference between someone who shows up to show up, versus someone who shows up on purpose. On purpose does not "go with the flow." Proactive absolutely does not sleep walk. Most of us glaze over or ignore the fact that being on purpose is a choice. It is. On purpose is a choice.

LOSERS, WINNERS AND EVERYONE ELSE

> *"It's a town full of losers, and I'm*
> *pulling out of here to win."*
>
> - "Thunder Road"
> by Bruce Springsteen

This next part is going to get uncomfortable. Here is where I lose friends. #Honesty

Stop for a moment and take inventory of most people that you personally know. Who is winning? Who is losing?

We all have certain people in our lives that are "losers." Honest, right? I'm not name calling, but I am categorizing. Welcome to our first category - the "Losers."

You know who the losers are. Things are always wrong. Complaining is a lifestyle. Unhappy is a hobby. Drama. The cup is always half empty, if there is even a cup at all. Well, would ya look at that? Someone stole their cup! I'm sure you'll read all about it on their Facebook Wall.

This is the loser category. Check. And for the record, the "loser" mindset is a choice as well, but I'll address that later. Moving on…

There is a second category, and it's larger (hopefully) then the last one we discussed. This is where you would place (mostly) everyone else. So, for the sake of a visual, who gets dumped into this category? Well, it's not the constantly down, complaining, loser candidate. The top achievers are not in this group, either.

This is the "Average" category.

The average group of people (Yes, I realize I'm not making many friends right now, but I didn't write this to waste *our* time) consists of the comfortable. There is no real fire or ambition, and that's okay because things are okay. There are 9-5 jobs that are not bad, but are not necessarily inspiring either. There is no zeal or ambition for any "unrealistic" goal or dream, but there is a constant thirst to binge watch that favorite show. Life is fine. It could always be better, but for the most part, it's fine. Autopilot. Got the visual? Good.

So we have this (hopefully) limited "loser" category (who by the way can *easily* advance to the average group), and the much larger "average" tier. Check.

Allow me to turn your attention to the group that most likely has the least amount of members. Ladies and gentlemen, I give you the "Winners."

Stop right here. The previous part was clearly uncomfortable. This next portion is down right ugly. Like your mama. Sorry (I had to lighten things up).

There is a saying that people love a winner. You think so, huh? Meh. Knock it off. Another lie. Want proof? Here it comes.

Let's look at professional sports for an example. Take football. I'll name a "popular" franchise that has one of the most loyal fan bases, but on the same token is one of the most hated organizations of all time.

The New England Patriots are winners. People hate them. H-A-T-E them. During Super Bowl 51, the entire country, excluding that little area in the far Northeast, was rooting for the Atlanta Falcons. In some interviews, I heard football fans say they would root for anyone other than the Patriots. Really? Anyone? Why?

Because they win. They have been to nine Super Bowls as an organization. That's more than any other of the thirty one remaining teams, and have won five Championships with Tom Brady as quarterback and Bill Belichick as head coach. Since the new millennium, they have absolutely dominated in most cases, regardless of what players come and go on their roster. As a matter of fact, over the years this squad has created a culture of taking unwanted, underutilized talent or players that other teams deemed too old, not skilled enough or had personal off field issues, turning them into refurbished, rejuvenated champions. There is literally a "next man up" mentality, being able to work with whatever moving parts they are utilizing and are known to have the team slogan "do your job."

What's not to love? They win. Do they win too much?

Maybe everyone doesn't "love a winner." Maybe everyone "loves a winner" if they don't win too much, or everyone "loves a winner" if they are an underdog and they win when they weren't supposed to.

Other than Division rival teams, do you know who hates the Cleveland Browns? Nobody. Why? There have been 52 Super Bowls. Forget winning one, the Browns have never APPEARED in one. For the most part, they are irrelevant. Sorry Cleveland. All love, just facts.

Maybe I won't schedule my book tour there. Regardless, if they ever do make a Super Bowl appearance, you can bet the country will be pulling for them because "everybody loves a winner, um…I mean…underdog."

Bottom line is this… popularity breeds contempt and people resent success. Why? Maybe because it exposes our own shortcomings and inadequacies. Friends, don't hate. Appreciate it.

ACTING AND NOT WAITING

*"To hell with circumstances. I create
opportunities."*

- Bruce Lee

Let's get back to being "on purpose." Do you think Patriots' owner Bob Kraft just kind of, sort of, created one of - if not THE greatest dynasty of all time in the history of all of professional sports by sleepwalking?

Do you think Coach Belichick just shows up and rolls with it? Does Tom Brady really just mosey in from the off-season with a tan in July and just decides to wing it? Does that really happen, or do they show up on purpose?

I'm pretty sure they show up on purpose.

I think they show up with laser beam focus, setting the pace as leaders of the team (and the league). I believe they raise the bar and have expectations not only for themselves, but for the entire supporting cast.

They are winners.

So back to you and your network. After all, your network is your net worth. We already identified and filled two of the three categories with the "loser" troop and that "average" squad. So, who are the winners? Who is in that elect group of people that you know who just seem to...win?

They are always leading the pack, aren't they? They radiate success and good fortune always shines on them. They are always winning.

Picture them? Good. Do you hate them? Hopefully not. If you do, do they deserve it? Maybe we can switch perspective and not only appreciate them for their victories, but learn from them and their winning techniques.

I 100 percent guarantee that you can step back and look at most - if not all of the winners in your life and bet safely on the fact that they are self starters.

They're not waiting. They're not hoping. They're not "winging it." They show up on purpose. They have an agenda. They're early. They're prepared. They're motivated. It's a mindset. It's a winning mindset.

All of that is. Words like prepared, motivated, and purposeful are not just words. They are real things. Those attributes are the foundation of what champions are made of and dynasties are founded on.

So, those winners - the ones you personally know? They didn't just wake up that morning and decide then that they were going to dominate everything in their path. That was on their mind the night before, all last week, last month. Put away that instinctive human resentment and appreciate their effort. It's a lifestyle.

There is an old saying. It reads: "How you do anything is how you do everything." I love that. It's true. Most old sayings are. That's why they're old. They've stood the test of time.

Ever notice how the winners are always productive? I didn't say "busy." I said productive. There's a difference. We are all busy these days. There is a difference between being "busy" catching up with the latest episode of "Dancing With The Stars" versus being productive.

How about this old saying: "If you want something done, give it to a busy person." That's true too. Winners are always busy being productive. They are never "bored." They have no time for it. Leave that for the half empties in the "loser" bracket. Ouch. If you are bored, go volunteer. I'm sure hungry, homeless, dying and hurting children, veterans or lonely elderly would love to connect with you on your down time.

Got your attention? Good.

Be a self starter. You must. Well, let me correct myself. You must if you want to win.

Lacey Lautenschlager was a featured guest on my web-based show. She received the "Spirit" award from her company at the yearly Global Training Conference in front of 15,000 people. That award represents someone who inspires, cares for others and lifts people up by their example and actions.

Lacey is a wife and a mother who not only runs her home-based business, but more times than not she does so alone. What about her husband you may ask? Well, he deploys for duty overseas. Frequently. With the Bomb Squad. He's not going to Guam with the volleyball team (Great - now I can't go to Cleveland *or* Guam). He is no stranger to desperate, violent, remote locations for unknown durations of time. Talk about stress.

In addition to the stress of having a hero husband who is fulfilling his long-distance military obligations, Lacey is a single parent. She is a parent to a special-needs child. Actually, she is a parent of and cares for two special-needs children.

When I asked Lacey how she musters the fortitude to get through her day, she referenced her grandmother that forever instilled a saying into her mind. Her grandmother would say "You can. You will. You must."

That's it. No "what ifs." No safety net. No fear. No excuses. She doesn't wait, she acts. She trained herself to self start daily. She makes it work good days, bad days, and everything in between. I'm sure it's not always pretty, but she does what she has to do.

Lacey is strong. Lacey is a self starter. She has to be. She has no choice.

Stop sleep walking. Open your eyes. Start showing up on purpose. Stop waiting for a cue. It's your time. Go be a self starter and take charge. Do you know who gets to make that decision? You!

Being on purpose is a choice, and I want to stop right here to applaud you. By reading this, you have already made that choice which means you are filling up, expanding and rising. If you are reading this, you already are self starting. Congrats! Keep going. Keep being on purpose. Keep moving towards winning.

Be a self starter. You can. You will. You must.

RANT #4

HEAL

For the most part, this book is geared more toward inspiration with less emphasis on empathy. However, I do believe in it and know that there is a time and place for it. If you are in need, now is the time and this is the place. My hope is that these words will serve you some comfort.

I know it hurts so bad. Being in the thick of it, you can't and don't care or want to see right now, but just know that you will heal.

I have a weekly show on Youtube called "Monday Mornings With Marc Hayford." The program showcases different guests who have pushed through their threshold of pain and have succeeded past barriers. They inspire others, they carry the ones who can't walk, and give vision to those who can't see.

In season 3, I featured a motivational speaker by the name of John O'Leary. John is the author of the book "On Fire." Do you know what the book is about? It's about John O'Leary being on fire. I mean the man was literally set on fire. Blown up. He should never have advanced out of childhood because the little boy who played with gasoline should be dead. But he's not.

To watch your baby suffer like that. His poor parents. I can't imagine the despondent, woeful daily living they endured.

During our live taped interview he took a sip from his bottled water. He used both hands to clench the bottle because he has no fingers. To me it was shocking. To him it is reality. Yet this man somehow writes and plays the piano.

Heal. You owe yourself that. But make sure you heal. Revive. Rejuvenate. Sometimes it feels like the circumstance is unrecoverable. Let time mend the scar.

Others will understand. Others can help. Others have been where you are right now. This isn't the end. Reach out and let someone know. Talk about the pain because there are those who want to help you and accompany you on your walk.

You will recover and healing will happen. Believe it. Harmony may not be right around the corner, but it is on the way. Exhale and fill yourself with peace. Learn to have gratitude and remember that for which you have to be thankful. Rest your heart. Have faith. Believe. Let time heal.

4

SPECIAL

*"Everybody is a genius. But if you judge a fish
by it's ability to climb a tree it will live it's life
believing that it is stupid."*

\- Albert Einstein

I want you to forget for a moment what you *think* you
know. Forget what you think you know about me, and
more importantly forget what you think you know about
you. When this chapter is all said and done, I hope that
I showcased a message that I believe needs to be heard.
I want to shed some light and bring a little perspective.

When I was growing up in northern New Jersey, I was
raised by a great Dad. He wasn't perfect, but he was a
great Dad. He was a Vietnam Veteran, who was way too
stressed out and smoked way too much. He didn't have
a college degree or what would be deemed as a stable
career. He wasn't very handy, and at times he could have
an explosive temper. I know I'm not describing the pic-
ture-perfect role model right now, but he was a great

Dad. What made him great was he loved us, protected us and always did his best for our family.

We never had a lot of nice things like some of the other families in the neighborhood. We didn't have a luxurious home. I had a bedroom that was literally probably the size of most people's bathrooms, and I shared that room with my brother. We had no front yard, just sidewalk and the sound of traffic three feet away from the main street. We didn't even have a front door. We had an alley that you would walk into to enter my house from the side. Trick Or Treaters hardly ever came, and when they did we were stunned. The view from our kitchen window was the other building next to us in the alley, so when I did homework my view were bricks and cinderblock, or other people staring back at me from their bathroom window. I grew up next to a bar - one of many in our town.

We could never afford a family vacation. I don't remember ever having one, as in never. As a matter of fact, there was a period in time when my father first became ill with multiple sclerosis and we didn't have a family car. Praise God for the Church who brought food to our home, so we wouldn't go hungry. It was embarrassing. But we ate, so despite how it made me feel, I was always thankful.

Regardless of circumstances, I still enjoyed my childhood. Despite tons of allergies and asthma (which I've since outgrown), I was healthy. I had friends. I had a life. One thing I did take for granted at the time and never really thought much of because I just accepted it for what it was, was the fact that my father always told me that I was "special."

Pump the brakes, friends. I didn't say "entitled" (because I'm not). I said "special."

I never found this necessarily impactful at the time, but as I think back over the years this was something my father instilled in me. I think I never viewed this as impactful in those times because he just told me that I was "special." That's it. It stopped there. He never told me *how* or *why* I was special. Maybe he didn't know how or why. Maybe he just knew and delivered the message that I was special.

He was right. I am.

And so are you.

As my father did with me decades ago, I am going to do with you right now. This isn't some "rah-rah" feel good campaign. The purpose of this chapter is to wake you up. This is to remind you - or show you - how valuable you really are. I am going to bring perspective to the fact that whether you believe it or not, YOU create an IMPACT.

Impact is powerful. You are powerful. You are impactful.

See, you carry energy. We all do. Whether you like it or not that energy is either going to offer some light to the world and lift others up, or becomes something that just takes up space becoming an obstacle for you and others. The good news is that you get to choose. What are *you* going to do with *your* energy? Your energy is a gift. *What* are you going to do with *your* gift? With whom are you going to share your energy? Who will receive your gift?

THE PERSON IN THE MIRROR

"Mirrors lie. They don't show you what's inside."
- Demi Lovato

How you see yourself is crucial. Paramount. Imperative. That is the energy that projects. How you view yourself - the confidence you do or do not have will speak volumes to the universe. I'm not suggesting the old "fake it 'till you make it" gimmick. I mean really visualizing and embracing your importance. That's important. Your vibe and energy will reverb volumes.

In a hospital I've been asked if I was the doctor. "No, I'm a visitor."

In schools I've been asked if I was the principal. "No, I'm a dad."

Act, breathe, eat, sleep, walk, talk, think…become as if. Your attire is important. Your posture is important. Your vocabulary is important. It's all important, but it starts with that inner energy that we all possess. Let that out!

One day, I was in a convenience shop of a gas station. While grabbing the item that I needed, I happened to overhear a conversation between the female employee behind the counter and a female customer from what I could tell was very, very rich.

Was she wealthy? She was definitely dressed nicely. But I don't mean rich with what was in her bank account. I'm talking about her essence. The atmosphere she created was one of abundance. The worker behind the counter? She on the other hand was poor. Poor in spirit.

"Yeah," she said. "So the guy says to me 'Oh are you somebody important' and I was like, who? Me? No, not really! And then the jerk just walked passed me and..."

I didn't hear anything else. All I needed to hear I already heard. "No. I'm not important" is what she said. Ouch.

Unfortunately, she was right. That was her first problem. How you see yourself is exactly how others will feel that energy and begin to see you also. That person in the mirror is important. Without him/her - the game is over! You matter!!

This ended with the "rich" woman serving the "poor" woman. It was magnificent.

"Yes you are!" She reassured. "You are a mother who is standing up for the rights and her beliefs for one of her children. You should be proud of your stance. Great job and don't ever apologize for doing the right thing! What would have happened if you weren't there?"

"I guess you're right," poor woman said. "I never saw it that way."

Sometimes it's nice to hear how valuable you are, and so important to realize that you actually count. "You are special." Thanks, Dad.

This scene ends with rich woman smiling at the employee, turning and smiling at me, and then leaving. No more words were necessary at this point. Just energy. The poor woman was taken back for a moment, simply staring at the register as if I wasn't even there, as she was trying to fully capture the understanding that she mattered. She may have just had what was her first ever deposit made into her self-esteem account. I approached the counter as the woman slowly looked up. We locked eyes in a vulnerable moment of silence.

"Just this latte, please." So anticlimactic.

YOUR PURPOSE

"The purpose of life is to find your gift. The meaning of life is to give it away."
- Pablo Picasso

Strong willed. Big mouth. To the point.

That's my mother. I'm not being disrespectful. Those are her own words describing herself. She's right. Unfortunately, when she describes herself, she leaves out some pretty important attributes to her character.

I would add persevering, caregiving, fighter and advocate to the list.

Barbara Hayford is forever taking care of someone, or something else. Sometimes, it is to a fault. The woman is unable to be still.

When I was 20 years old, I joined the United States Air Force. It was at that moment in basic training that I came to the harsh reality that I had no clue as how to make my bed, cook a meal or do a load of my own laundry. Why would I? I would never have the chance or the need to, because Mom would do it. Yes, I was borderline pathetic.

As I mentioned earlier, when my father went down with MS our world changed drastically. With my brother being too young, Mom and I grabbed whatever jobs we could, usually two or three different ones simultaneously to keep our heads above water. One of the jobs was with a cleaning company scrubbing beer and vomit off of floors and toilets of some of the North Jersey bars and strip clubs. This woman did whatever it took, to make us make it.

Years later as Dad's decline became aggressive, it was clear she needed help for and with him. But my Mom is different. When some of the outside entities tried to give basic medical assistance to him, it wasn't good enough for her. She knew sticking him in a hospital to rot wasn't something he wanted, or what she would accept. She decided to be the primary caregiver. She wasn't a nurse, she wasn't a doctor, and she wasn't qualified, but like I said, she was and still is persevering, caregiving, fighting and an advocate.

Herds of agencies and assistants came in and went out of our home. If they went out, it was because she kicked them out. Too rough with dad or not rough enough? Get out. You don't speak English well and can't communicate? Get out. You're gonna call your boyfriend from the house phone while still on the clock? Hang up. Get out.

There was nobody on the planet who could have taken care of my then bedridden father as well as my mother did. She changed diapers, gave the best meals and incentives to someone who was just done with life, and fought, and fought, and fought for his rights and the absolute best assistance he could get. I am absolutely convinced that as much as they got on each other's nerves sometimes, this woman added another decade of life to David D. Hayford Jr.

Dad passed away on January 1, 2007. I don't look at New Year's Day as somber. I view it as liberation. My father was released from a dreadful disease. When I do see him again, he won't be broken, debilitated and weak. He will be then and is now free.

As far as Mom, I don't know where she gets it. Maybe it was that rough environment of northern New Jersey. Maybe it had to do with the trying life experiences. I do know that some of my character for better or worse, is definitely inherited and instilled from my mother.

We all have a purpose. It doesn't necessarily mean winning, achieving or getting something. Sometimes it means giving. Sometimes it means giving yourself.

Strong willed? Big mouth? To the point? Sure.

Giver? Absolutely. If a statue is ever erected to showcase a giver, just make sure it is of my Mom.

YOUR GIFTS

"Many people die at 25 and aren't buried until 75."

- Benjamin Franklin

Stuff happens. It happens to all of us. Regardless of your education level, social status, financial state - life is hard and challenges will come. If they haven't yet, they will. It's not a matter of if, it's a matter of when. Expect it. These challenges do not discriminate, so whether you are part of the family that is seeking shelter for the night or you live in that mansion on the elite side of town, garbage is going to get thrown at you. Sometimes it will come at you from all sides, all at once.

But you are still here. Just like this message I am delivering to you, you are ALIVE. No matter what you've gone through in your past or what your current situation is, you are reading or hearing these words. That means YOU have purpose. You matter. Your story, your work isn't finished yet. I'll say it again. You have purpose. If you have purpose, you matter. If you matter, you have purpose. Recognize it.

Somewhere on this enormous merry-go-round, you are needed. You are needed not to simply exist, but to share. Share what? Share yourself. Your gifts, your talents, the special stuff, the weird stuff, your spirit - that's needed. The universe needs that. The universe needs you. Don't believe that? That's the problem. Let's fix it.

I DJ private events. I absolutely love it. In my line of work over the years, I've had the distinct pleasure of playing a role in so many incredible weddings where I can say I was there when "happily ever after" actually started. I've done all the surprise birthday parties, especially the "significant ones" where the birthday age ended with a zero. I was there for those sweet sixteen celebrations where I helped make that girl feel special. I've done the private events for - literally - heroes such as firefighters, police and military. The occasions where funds were raised and awareness was created, the times when communities came together to either heal or celebrate, the events for the schools where the children or teens had a blast in a safe, appropriate environment, and everything else in and between is where you could find me over the years with two speakers, a mixer and a microphone.

The milestones. The celebrations. The memories. I love what I do because simply put, I have the dubious honor of taking part in some of the absolute greatest and most unforgettable moments in people's lives. I add value to their event and in return I receive the blessings of what it feels like when you share yourself and your gifts. That's when you really feel like you matter. When you live and become that purpose.

A while back, I was asked to perform at a non competitive pageant/fashion show. I have a soft spot in my heart for these types of events and the giving spirit of the people who run them. Through the years, I have witnessed firsthand through my own daughter what this can do for little girls.

For starters, the network of friends and the bond these children can make is so special. Next, for so many (especially first timers) these little girls get to experience what it feels like to truly become a princess. I think at least once in their lives every little girl should have the experience of what it is like to have someone doting on you.

Having your hair done, makeup put on just right, along with that perfect gown and special pair of shoes is a slice of Heaven for them. It's absolutely precious.

Now that decade and a half plus resume detailing almost every type of function known to humanity that I've ever performed at was about to grow. This was going to be my first runway event, and I have to tell you that I was excited. My daughter Jayda was taking part in it, my wife was going to attend, and I was very much looking forward to enhancing it from start to finish.

I must tell you about another skillset that I bring to the table as it is important in this story, and that is that I am a master of ceremonies. I enjoy the art of speaking, and I feel when a solid DJ can not only run the itinerary but also host and announce well it completely pulls the banquet together and puts it over the top.

However, on this particular occasion, that would not be needed from me. I was being brought in to keep the flow moving, the beats dropping and the music to be a presence but not overpowering. Turns out there already was an emcee. Sort of.

While setting up for the event, I quickly realized there were a handful of ladies who volunteered to help out behind, and not so behind the scenes. One woman in particular stood out to me more than the others. She appeared to be in her mid-fifties, not very self-assured and clearly not experienced or comfortable with performing the duties of announcing or public speaking. But she was dutiful. "Carol" was a tornado of setting up the room, moving decorations from parking lot to the second floor and eager to move to the next task.

Prior to the event, I introduced myself and informed that I would be happy to assist in anyway once we got rolling. Noticing there were prizes and raffles, I was assuming I was going to be announcing all the info as usual, until Carol informed me that *she* was asked to do all the announcing during the event. Okay then.

Once the fashion show kicked off, it was clear from the opening moments that Carol was not a professional speaker. Like, not at all. There were amateurish moments of prolonged silence, times of stumbling over what was needing to be announced, and instances of overall awkwardness. Knowing my level of expectation, I was internally cringing.

After the first round of her speaking to the crowd, she returned the microphone to me and I said to her "Good job." Now, truth be told it wasn't actually a "good job." Well, hold on. It wasn't a good job for someone with experience like myself, but Carol was clearly not a pro, this was absolutely her first time and from that angle it wasn't terrible. It was a good job. For her.

She smiled, handed the mic over and said "I'm done. I was so nervous!"

Hmm. I didn't get that. The annoying, critiquing, professional, Type A part of me viewed indecisiveness with an awkward and choppy delivery, but I didn't see nervous.

As Carol was walking away, I quickly caught up to her and tapped her shoulder. Shouting over my speaker dropping bass just a few feet behind me, I told her that if she was nervous I didn't recognize that, the crowd didn't recognize that, and that she should "Keep going." She smiled and walked away.

Throughout the event as droves of little girls walked the red carpet in all their glory, Carol had the opportunity to speak more, and often. She had to because I refused. It was clear that the more she did it, the more comfortable she became. At one point, she even laughed, motioned to the mic and said "You're not getting this back!" I didn't want it back, because Carol was starting to really, really do a good job.

When all was said and done, the show was a success. The girls and their families had the best time, people walked away with prizes, and everyone was happy. As for Carol, she discovered something. From that quick journey of uncertainty to comfort, she gained the confidence to overcome a fear and embrace something new. She learned something about herself that day. She may have never been actively taught it, and no one may have ever guided her to think it was a possibility, but while showing up to serve, Carol left realizing something meaningful. She learned that she matters and she has a talent. She has purpose. She is special.

Her undiscovered gifts, her unforeseen talents, the special stuff, the weird stuff, her spirit - the universe needed it. I know I'll probably see…scratch that. I know I'll probably *work* with her again. That afternoon was not a one and done.

After fifty-five years, someone realized that their work and their story isn't finished yet. If she discovered her gifts after half a century, you can too. The universe needs you. Believe it. Share it. Let it out.

RANT #5

———

SURPRISE

Heeeeey…you've made it. Congrats! You are more than halfway through this saga. Thanks for toughing it out. Now, let's get to it and do some real tough sledding.

SURPRISE!

In the opening lines from Tears For Fears number 1 smash hit from 1985, "Everybody Wants To Rule The World", they sing "*Welcome to your life. There's no turning back.*"

Try to remember back when you were old enough to recognize things. Mommy and Daddy (if you were lucky enough to have both or even one of them), your favorite toy or pet, and familiar surroundings all feel safe and warm. The family couch you would sit on, any old TV shows and maybe some favorite video games may come to mind too. Got that picture, that nostalgia in your mind? Okay, good.

Surprise! Here we are. Present day. Real circumstances. The past is just that. The past. As sweet as it was, it's now wiped away. So what now? How did you get here? Do you wish you were somebody else? Do you hate who you are? Are you ready to check out? Are you that 15-year-old high school kid who is getting cyber bullied by a bunch of people who won't matter soon in adulthood, or am I speaking to the 55-year-old salesman who is still in some kind of financial debt that probably won't actually matter in years to come?

Reality. You are here. You are STILL here. You are not here to suffer and slowly dissipate. You are not here to end things abruptly. You are not here to drag others down with you. You were made to THRIVE. You were made to help. You are gifted.

Surprise! Things didn't shape up the way you thought they would from your fifth grade imagination. Your initial dreams didn't magically pull the universe together to make stars align exactly the way you wanted. You got sucked into what everybody else does. Life.

Deal. Understand. Do NOT accept. Don't get tired on me. No, no, friends. We have work to do, and you are needed. You are way too valuable to just exist and tolerate. You were made to make a difference.

So, surprise! You're not going anywhere yet, except forward and up. Prepare to get prepared. Create some amazing things and surprise others. Read on. Let's go.

5

PLAYING TO WIN

"Success is a lousy teacher. It seduces smart people into thinking they can't lose."

- Bill Gates

I remember standing in center field as a 9 year old for a very anticipated Friday Night under-the-lights Little League baseball game. It was very anticipated, because at the time we (Variety Drug) had one of the worst records in the league while the Wallington Lanes were on a tear blazing through anything in their path. This one had massacre written all over it. It was ridiculous. The scoreboard read "Visitor" 35 and "Home" 3. We, obviously, were Home. 35 to 3. What a circus. I was embarrassed. I was angry. No, I was pissed. But I was never broken.

This wasn't the "we don't keep score" era to "protect" feelings. I had some feelings. The feelings that I had left weren't bruised, they were boiling.

In between watching pitches from that solitary center field position, I watched people that were muddling around the stands and parking lot. It looked like they were there more for a social event instead of a competitive baseball game to cheer the kids. I couldn't blame them. We didn't give them anything to cheer about.

It was embarrassing. It was disrespectful. I didn't like it. I learned something that day. I learned that I don't like to lose.

I didn't say that I was a sore loser. I said I don't like to lose. Who does? Do you? If you say yes, you're lying. Everyone loses now and again. It's life. But you don't have to like it. You *shouldn't* like it.

They finally stopped the game because of the score. I don't even remember what it was. To the 9-year-old me, that was the worst part. Shameful. That night battle scars grew on my heart and battle lines were drawn in my mind. That was the unforeseen beauty of it all. I woke up.

I do not need therapy from that experience. I wasn't coddled and rocked to sleep post game. We played like garbage, got crushed and that's that. There was no 12-run rule for me and my underoo-wearing teammates that night, and there isn't one out here in this jungle we call life.

Here comes the debate, but to me there really isn't one. I'm not the participation trophy guy, and I'm absolutely not the "don't keep score" guy either. Let's say ten of us go in for a job interview where there is one position available. Nine are going home. That's it. Should we offer cupcakes and a "Congrats On Your 7th Place Ranking For The Position" certificate? Maybe we should have separate participation trophies for the nine who have to go find employment somewhere else. Would that make them feel better? Is that ridiculous? It is? That's what we are teaching our children. While the nine stunned, non selected candidates are standing around crying, would they be better off: A) filing a complaint, holding their breath and asking to talk to the manager's manager, or B) Sucking it up, getting back in the trenches, and creating the next opportunity so they can nail a job? Too harsh, right? Makes sense though, right? Don't shoot the messenger. Eat or be eaten out here.

Today I see too many that are groomed to be protected and self-entitled, or those that think they are doomed right out of the gate before they ever get started. It's all wrong. I see those that think they have no chance at all, and they muddle through daily because, well… that's life. They never realize what an impact they can make. I see others who honestly believe they are the next superstar of the galaxy when they haven't done anything to earn it. They can just show up and it's all good. Both of these groups were either the recipients of too many hugs, or not enough hugs. There is a middle ground. Let's do real talk.

GO FOR IT

"I've failed over and over and over again in my life. And that is why I succeed."

\- Michael Jordan

In the "Self Starting" Chapter, I talked about winners. I personally know, and know of many successful entrepreneurs. I have also seen just as many pretenders who come and go with the seasons.

Do you want to know what makes the difference for the very top, upper echelon of the winners? Their secret? Shhhhh. Don't tell anyone. Here it is...

They are NOT afraid to lose.

They will take *calculated* risks and play to win. That doesn't mean they are bullet proof, super courageous or they throw caution into the wind like a gambling maniac. It means they do not play to lose, they simply play to win.

See, any legitimate player has already lost - probably more than a few times - and probably big, too. This isn't a failure, and it isn't a weakness. It means they have the strength and advantage of experience. What comes with that is the wherewithal that they are not afraid to lose like the unscaved, because they have already lost.

The big difference for the top players is they KNOW they are going to win again. They don't think, they know that if they built something once that collapsed, they can build and rise again.

There are some who may boast of a squeaky clean winning track record, but there is a problem with that. If you have never lost, you have never tried. Playing from a safe place means you ARE afraid to lose, and playing not to lose instead of striving to win will usually cause you to…well, lose.

Remember how in the Chapter "Self Starting" I showcased how being comfortable is dangerous? Equally dangerous is playing not to lose or the scarcity mindset. This isn't a fairy tale. What you project is exactly what you receive back. If you think small and play small, you win small. Maybe. If you win at all. The ones who are the real deal go for it. They think more, give more, go for more, and subsequently have more. Play big, friends.

SEEK OPPORTUNITY

"Being realistic is the most commonly traveled road to mediocrity."

\- Will Smith

Obviously, this doesn't apply across the board or in every single case. However, have you ever noticed that some people are in the position that they are in for a reason?

The hungry, the ambitious and the successful all seek opportunity. Eyes wide open. Consistently. Winners don't have their heads in the sand, they are paying attention.

Nine out of ten times they are capitalizing on their opportunities, and they parlay them into more opportunities.

Deciding to create my own DJ company allowed me to get my foot in the door with professional wrestling. Professional wrestling gave me the connections I needed to become a co-owner of an arena football team. The entertaining aspect of DJing, wrestling and arena football helped me cultivate showmanship where I was able to be a frontman for a touring, arena playing Christian rock band. I wasn't even a trained vocalist, but I sought the opportunity, hired vocal coaches (plural) and became one. Do yourself a favor and seek one. Not a vocal coach, an opportunity. If you can't find one, create one!

Some will claim to be skeptical. They affirm it like it's an award they received. They are borderline proud of it.

There is a known adage that states: "Skepticism will keep you broke." It's true. I've seen it firsthand. I have witnessed individuals who have been reached out to and given incredible opportunities. On some occasions, these people *needed* an opportunity - any opportunity - let alone an incredible one. So many times I've seen that door close, the opportunity is gone and the person who was offered it is still in the same place as they were before they were offered it in the first place.

It can be fear, ignorance, laziness (a big one today), scarcity mindset, too finicky, too particular, no focus, skepticism or any other reason, the answer to the offer was "No." Same position. Same issue. Same story.

Successful people say yes. Don't take it from me. Take it from the icons.

Warren Buffet is a billionaire investor. In 2017, he was recognized as the second wealthiest person in the world. His advice? "Opportunities come infrequently. When it rains gold, put out the bucket, not the thimble."

Billionaire Sir Richard Branson who founded Virgin Group (which controls more than 400 companies) also had thoughts on this. He said, "If someone offers you an amazing opportunity and you're not sure you can do it, say yes - then learn how to do it later."

Billionaire Chief Operating Officer of Facebook Sheryl Sandberg says, "If you're offered a seat on a rocket ship, don't ask what seat. Just get on."

Seek an opportunity. Get on the freakin' rocket ship and start learning to say yes. All the winners are doing it.

STOP STOPPING

Stop it! Stop it! Stop it already!

Why do we play so small? Why do we get in our own way? Why do we allow the junk that comes into our head to stay there? Why do we choose to fly so low to the ground and prevent ourselves from reaching our potential to soar? Are we that concerned with what anyone else thinks or says?

Stop doing yourself a disservice. Stop stopping yourself!

Do you know that Jimi Hendrix constantly had to be reassured that his look was "cool?" We're talking Hendrix - one of the greatest and most innovative guitar players of all time who defined a psychedelic era with his look alone. He was worried about how he would be perceived. Who would have thought?

Do you know when you're 90 years old and reflecting back on life what you really won't care about - or even remember? You won't care about that kid - what's her name - from school that gave you a hard time. You won't have any anxiety from the coworker who was judgmental but couldn't get their own life straight. You won't stress about the people who doubted you. You won't even remember their names or faces.

But, you will have to live with regret. You will have to live with regret if you keep holding back because of your everyday uncertainty. When it's all said and done, don't set yourself up for dissatisfaction of regret and remorse of what could have been because you never played all out. Live! Now!

Walk boldly. Set trends. Be yourself. Don't judge. Ignite others. Welcome the journey. Enjoy the growth. Appreciate the struggle. Screw the critics. Allow yourself to fly.

Quit quitting. Stop Stopping. Stop stopping yourself so you can start doing you and live the life that you deserve!

6

YOUR HEAD, YOUR HEART, YOUR HUSTLE

*"I remained too much inside my head
and ended up losing my mind."*

- Edgar Allen Poe

"FYI get out of your head, get off your rear and go create the rest of your life today. In case you needed to hear it."

That's a text message I sent earlier this year on a Monday morning. It was to a long-time friend of more than 30 years who was fresh from getting laid off just 72 hours before. He was completely blindsided. Two kids, a wife, a home, and now no job. Wow. Have a nice weekend.

I can imagine what that first Monday felt like. Everyone is on the go, his wife leaves for work, his boys off to school, and then…nothing. Silence. Alone. Alone in that house with all the emptiness, the feel of worthlessness, the fear of uncertainty of any type of future. I'm sure there was an unyielding feeling of being in a familiar setting at an unfamiliar time. While the world hustled and bustled and was obliviously off to grind out their week, my friend was in an eerily quiet house, on an unplanned second cup of coffee, with a mirror.

He got to stare into that mirror and contemplate so much. "What now?" "Why me?" "Where do I go from here?" "Am I worthy?" "Can I do this?"

It can be so confusing, depressing and shameful to be in that spot. It wasn't his fault that the company was downsizing, offshoring his job, having cutbacks or replacing his position with some form of modern automation. But that actuality cannot replace the worrisome heaviness that he must have felt knowing that he needs to produce without a clue of where to take the next unexpected step. That position can make a man feel hopeless and insignificant.

I've seen many people play that game before. It's hard to watch. Witnessing experienced, wordly men and women fall back into a lesser version of themselves can be paralyzing. I personally know of someone who woke up, got dressed in business attire and left daily for work. This person was jobless for months during that duration but didn't want their spouse to know. They were too humiliated to let anyone know that they were unemployed. Seeing someone you know or care about trying to navigate throughout the fog of an unpredictable future can be humbling and make you thankful for your position in life.

THE HEAD

"The longest journey you will ever take is the 18 inches from your head to your heart."
                                                              - Unknown

Embarrassed. Uncertain. Depressed. Ladies and gentlemen, welcome to the head.

Our minds are so powerful, so untapped and always thirsting for more. Our minds are going even when we aren't. This, however, is not always necessarily to our benefit. Your brain is virtually a playground ranging from ideas, emotions, concerns, thoughts, beliefs and dreams. It is so robust yet can be such an enemy if not harnessed appropriately, just like a horse in the wild. Train the horse and you'll find major benefit. Don't train the horse and expect to be tossed off and injured. I can hear author of "Funny Side Up," Rita Davenport, say "Mind your mind." Thanks for the advice, Rita.

Stress will make you stupid. This isn't slang, this is fact. Emotions like anxiety, depression, panic and anger rarely help anyone make clear, rational decisions. How many times have you been in "the moment" and needed to apologize to someone later? We all have those moments, but it's about limiting them to only a moment and then standing back up. Every party comes to an end (I should know, I'm a DJ), and that especially counts for the pity party.

Many people deal with situations such as these differently. Some deal by not dealing. Like, at all. That's the mindset of knowing what you know. Ego. Rationale. I should know.

December of 2002 my wife and I were handed an important decision to make. We were deciding if we were going to pay our bills or celebrate Christmas. How about that? I was previously told by my employers before a vicious, first round of layoffs that I should be "thankful" as I had a "good" job. Thank you corporate America.

Christina is the hardest working person I know, and I know a lot of people. She has an appetite for ambition that runs circles around most. That particular Holiday season she was the stay at home mom for our 1-1/2-year-old son Kane, while 7 months pregnant with our soon-to-be baby girl, Jayda. Who cried. Consistently. Constantly. Inconsolably. Not Christina, Jayda. That's a whole separate book in itself. Regardless, we were down to one income - mine - and it wasn't getting the job done. Not like we needed it to, anyway.

Christina was turned onto another (Yes, we were approached and dabbled before) network marketing opportunity. This one wasn't like the others before. The products were trending, the products were consumable (which means repeat sales and residual income), and the company was poised to go global. Everything made sense.

I said no. Emphatically.

Let me play that back for you. One income. Drowning financially. Paycheck to paycheck. Holidays. Stress. We needed something. Anything.

I said no. Bonehead.

In my mind, I already had my job, my other venture hadn't completely taken off yet (more on that in a moment), and I wasn't educated on the future or the power of network marketing. I saw dated and failed ventures from the '80s verses the mobile, global businesses that we are seeing today. I had poor vision. Despite my perception (or lack thereof), my wife didn't, and she went for it. She wasn't going against my wishes, I had more of a "Do it if you want to, but I don't want to" attitude.

She did. Remember her work ethic that I spoke of? Her decision propelled us enough financially to not only get through that Holiday season, but by the summer of 2003 Christina matched what I was making in corporate America. When my youngest boy, Harrison, was born in 2005 she reached the top level of management in the pay scale where she still stands today. Her monthly commission check consistently quadrupled what I was making at my full time systems analyst job. So, I took paternity leave and never went back. I think they're still looking for me as I speak. I wonder if I got laid off yet.

I want to take this moment to publicly admit to my wife, all of you, and the rest of the universe that I was stupid. I wasn't stupid because I made the decision that I made, I was being foolish because I made the decision without being informed. I didn't know what I was saying "no" to. I knew better. That's dangerous. Christina, you were right and I was wrong. What else is new? Boy, that was painful.

Despite unforeseen misfortune, I see many that have constant misfortune. I believe some people (not everyone) are in the position that they are for a reason. I have personally experienced reaching out to some with an opportunity, knowing that not only did they need one, but that with a little effort, they would actually be good at it and it would be good for them.

No response. Voicemail. Unanswered text messages. Excuses. They'll think about it. Crickets.

Two years later these individuals are in the same position or worse. A successful person may not always say "yes," but a successful person will absolutely keep an open mind, and usually take a look. Proverbs 3:5 tells us: "Lean not on your own understanding." Don't think you know better like I did. Do your homework and get out of your head.

YOUR HEART

"I'm proud of my heart. It's been played, stabbed, cheated, burned and broken, but somehow it still works."

- unknown

I've actually seen some videos online with some of the these non-credentialed, self-proclaimed, self-righteous, somber experts who advise you to "not follow your passion." Ah, I gotcha. Follow your head, not your heart. They're correct.

They're correct if you want to take that advice so you can create a daily life of mundane where you are required to produce in an environment that you may potentially detest. They're so spot on if you are looking to create a lifestyle where you work for someone who did follow their passion. This is the voice of experience. I did that for years myself. I was dying inside. That's not living, that's existing. *That* is dismal.

Since my childhood and way before the time of MP3s and now dated compact discs, I was enamored with music. One Christmas, Santa brought a few shoeboxes of vinyl 45 records. They were all original records from Elvis, Sinatra, The Beach Boys, The Jackson Five - all of Motown, actually.

To this day, I still have hundreds of records from the '50s, '60s, '70s and '80s. I have no idea what they are worth but maybe someday one of my great-great-grandkids will. If you are one of them reading this, you're welcome and great-great-grandpa loves you.

I remember being a kid and putting on my Dad's headphones that were way too large to be comfortable while I watched him place the massive reel to reel analogue tapes on the tape deck. The dials were fat and clumsy, the sound was perfectly imperfect and it was beautiful.

As I got older, I had a stint with albums. My first one was the Australian's own Men At Work with "Business As Usual" which had their early '80s pop smash "Down Under." Then I liked "Karma Chameleon" so I purchased Culture Club's "Colour By Numbers." It was the '80s, don't judge me.

The breakthrough of MTV and those cheesy early day videos along with my Sony Walkman turned me onto all modern genres which was the game changer. It wasn't too long until I graduated to my AM/FM dual cassette tape deck "boombox." All the parachute-pants-wearing breakdancers had one. I never wore parachute pants, I couldn't breakdance, but I had one anyway. It was huge. It was obnoxious. It was magical.

In my lifetime, I've been to literally hundreds of concerts ranging from Woodstock to symphonies, to body surfing, the mosh pit, nosebleed cheap seats, general admission and the center front row. My first and greatest concert experience was my first, last and only concert experience with the man that turned me onto music in the first place - my Dad.

In the summer of 1985 at the New Jersey Meadowlands (specifically Giants Stadium), we together experienced the 4-1/2 hour, no opening act show of Bruce Springsteen and the E Street Band. Packed to the rafters as they say, we were at top level seating where the bass was so forceful I felt the pressure of it pounding on my chest. Surrounded by a gang of bikers who unveiled a humongous American Flag that we all played part in holding and waving, I just remember an ongoing party for the ages. I was hooked. As far as concert going these days, I do the same with my multi instrument playing musician teenage son, Kane. The only difference is that there was a first concert, someday there will be a last concert, but there is never an only concert. We go all the time.

Back then, every Sunday morning was on lockdown as I would listen to "American Top 40" hosted by Casey Kasem. I would keep a log. No, really. Each week, I would sit there with a pen and a pad and annotate the top 10 biggest mover and shaker hits of the country. Have you heard that writing something helps you remember it? Well it does. How else would I remember that Til Tuesday's hit "Voices Carry" hit number 8 on the Billboard Charts back in 1985?

With his familiar voice and never-ending factual statistics, Casey Kasem brought me to my safe, happy place. One week back in 1987, he read my "Long Distance Dedication" letter that I mailed in and played Bon Jovi's "Livin' On A Prayer." I was blown away! I still have the recording on a cassette tape. I'm just not sure what I can play it on these days so I can hear it.

Do you now understand when I say that I love music, that I have a passion for music, that I mean it? For me, it's not only nostalgia, it's my foundation.

Let's put my "foundation" and my "passion" on hold. We need to, because that's exactly what I did. Life happens, man. You can get kicked around, find yourself in situations you have never anticipated, on and on and on.

After graduating high school, I found myself doing full time security at the same Giants Stadium where where my Dad and I rocked out to "the Boss" just five years earlier. Many things changed in my life since that experience, and although I liked hanging around the New York Football Giants, it wasn't my life calling.

Neither was the single year that I attended Kean College in 1990-91. It wasn't my calling for two reasons. The first reason was I simply wasn't prepared or built for college. Too many books, not enough pictures. The second reason was we simply couldn't afford it. Not even a little bit. The disaster of the family car that I was driving back and forth to get there everyday on the New Jersey Parkway was a donation from a family who helped us out. When Dad's multiple sclerosis went full blown, my mom and I were unprepared and unexpectedly became the providers for the household. At the time, wealthy executive tycoons we were not. Already being a family from "down the hill," I was unfortunately all too familiar with the Church bringing us meals from time to time. So appreciative for giving souls, I was still nauseated that we were charity. But we fought on.

Get me outta there. Fast forward that tape deck of life a little bit, please. That's enough. Hit stop. Press play.

Wait. I'm in Korea? Oh, right. The Air Force. The food was great and I loved listening to Nirvana, but...hit "FF" just a little more. That should be good. Hit stop. Push play.

Where am I and why am I wearing a postal uniform? Puff Daddy is on the radio? It's the late 1990s? Please, hit fast forward again - Now! Okay, hit stop. Now you can press play. Perfect.

The year is now 2000 and I'm all grown up. I have a good life. I have a wife. We have a home. There's a complete family with children happening soon. I have a job. But I also personally have no outlet. My position? Not hurting, but unfulfilled.

You buy that car, to get to that job, to leave that house that you are paying for that you can't be at because you're at your job, which pays for your car, that gets you to that job, which pays for that house that is empty while you're at that job...you get it.

That was me. Bills. Responsibility. Adulting. Life. Yuck. You gotta eat, right? Of course you do. But that doesn't mean the day to day has to be miserable. Not if you keep your passion. Not if you don't lose your heart.

So there I was. Sitting in traffic like I did everyday on the commute home from work. I'm mindlessly staring out the window, hypnotically, as I did most days while I sat in that gridlock. Same commute. Same drive. Same trees. Same roads. Everyday. On that particular day, something caught my attention. Something new. As I was slowly inching closer to my destination of home, I noticed off in the distance that dilapidated sign of the bowling alley. I've passed this place over and over but never stepped foot in it. The sign hanging outside read "DJ Wanted."

Not a chef. Not a cashier. Not the alley waxing manager or head ball cleaner. They needed a DJ!

My heart came alive. I shook the cobwebs away. I started to feel the butterflies of excitement. On the other hand, there was a problem. The head. My head. All the commonsensical logic started presenting facts as to why I should had never even bother applying in the first place. And it all made sense.

"Yes. You have a zillion CDs, but you have no DJ equipment. You've never DJ'd before. Well, maybe you messed around at a party, but you have no *real* experience. They're looking for someone who actually *knows* what they're doing. You're 28 years old. You're almost 30! That's as ridiculous as DJing when you're 40. Plus you're losing your hair. Dude, it's about image. Keep your day job. It's over."

Sometimes we talk ourselves out of something before we even give ourselves a chance to get started. Many times the very thing we are running from is what we've created in our own mind. That's the head for you, rational and reasoning all the potential unlikely scenarios. Stupid head.

This 18-inch battle between my head waging war with my heart was all happening as my window of opportunity was quickly closing. I was passing the entrance to the parking lot and all I could think was "You're not qualified. They probably have someone by now anyway. Just go home and have dinner."

My head was so right. It just made complete sense. It was realistic and washed away all that crazy impulsiveness.

Then after a moment of silence, I had clarity. I heard one word.

"Go."

That's what my heart said. That's what I did.

I walked in and sat with the manager. After some chit chat he asked "So Matt - "

"It's Marc…"

"Right. Marc…what would you play if you were to spin here?"

"Weeell…" I said as my blank mind started racing.

At this moment in time I'm really not prepared, I have no playlist, I'm technically not even a DJ. Absolutely looking to stall, my head wants to chime in with "See? This is just wasting everyone's time. You should've just went home."

Clearly, my head wasn't looking to offer any help here. So I stayed with, and spoke from my heart.

"What would I spin? Well…I can't really say… becauuuuse…I'm thinking I would play to the crowd. I would play what I like, and I like everything" I said. He leaned in.

I continued with "I would mix it up to keep it fresh and roll with it. I'm not a fan of the guy or girl that plays the same sound or genre over and over to keep it safe. I would take chances. I would probably start with a classic rock staple, some current top 40, drop Biggie, bounce back to motown and then flow over to some current hip-hop. Usher, Led Zeppelin, James Brown and Pink all sound like a solid start. Oh and then Prodigy. I'd definitely have to drop Prodigy. And then -"

"Okay" he interrupted, extending his hand. "See you Saturday Night!"

"This Saturday?" I was in shock. I was the scheduled DJ. Was I actually ready for it? I guess we were about to find out. Thank you, heart!

We worked out the fine details of pay, oh and that little issue regarding me not having equipment. I used their house system while all the music was provided by me. Since the era of technology forced me to move from cassettes to compact disks, I accumulated tons of CDs. I had thousands. Actually, I still do.

That Saturday night was special. I spent 72 hours before it went down and called everyone I knew. I didn't text them - because texting didn't exist yet. I busted my tail to prep possible playlists and contests, and it was a success. I was told that was the most packed evening that the Phoenixville Lanes had seen for years. There was energy. I was sweating. I ripped the roof off of it.

When the night was over and I was leaving with my crates, the staff gave me a standing ovation with the manager yelling "Finally we got a real DJ!" And they did, every Saturday Night for close to a year.

I started a following. I invested in my own equipment. I upgraded when it was time to go digital. I started to pop. That was 18 years ago since I started. Today, the Phoenixville Lanes are long gone, but my business is not.

Sometimes I book as far out as two years in advance, and other than my loosely maintained "DJ Kinghayf" Facebook page, I don't advertise. I'm all word of mouth.

I'm not playing in bowling alleys or bars anymore, either. To be clear there is absolutely nothing wrong with that. My business has just evolved. Today I'm finding myself doing private events such as weddings, corporate functions, parties, proms, reunions, runways and anywhere there is a need for booty shakin', earth quakin', bottle poppin', party rockin', and never stoppin'. The "Self Proclaimed, Undisputed, Greatest DJ On Aaaaall Of The East Coast" will be at a dance floor near you!

Sorry. Sometimes I get excited.

The moral of the story? Hurry and book me now! Well, not really, but…the moral of the story is that you must follow your heart. You need to follow your passion. And then (the important part) you need to work it like your livelihood depends on it, because it just might. Follow your dream.

All those really smart, rational people who will explain away as to why you need to not bother to "follow your dreams" (seriously?) need to go be miserable by themselves. Glad I didn't listen to them, or I'd still be miserable. In that office with no windows. Nah, I'd probably be miserable and laid off by now instead.

You know the saying "If you love what you do, you'll never work a day in your life?" That's a lie. You will. I do. Sometimes, I run myself into the ground doing it, but it's something I love to do. It's a much better quality of life than when I was in that cubicle drooling and daydreaming without a window to look out. I'm not trying to beat you down if you're in a cubicle. You may love what you do. If so, fantastic. If not, I'm reminding you there is more for you if you go out and get it.

I don't know what your bowling alley parking lot, or your dream is. Maybe it's to be a belly dance instructor. Maybe it is to be a competitive eater in the 50-and-over category. It really doesn't matter. What does matter is that we are not promised another minute. So don't waste it. Follow your heart. Go for your dream. Don't miss the turn into that parking lot. Turn in and park. Introduce yourself to your destiny.

Then it begins. And this is the most important part. Get ready to work it. With work, your passion can become a lifestyle. Without work, it will stay a hobby. You choose.

THE HUSTLE

"You lollygag the ball around the infield. You lollygag your way down to first. You lollygag in and out of the dugout. Do you know what that makes you? Lollygaggers!"

- Bull Durham

No time to lollygag here. Not when you gotta hustle. And you gotta hustle.

Everyone has strengths, and everyone has weaknesses. I think a strength is knowing your weakness and a weakness is not knowing your strength. There are many, many things that I am *not* good at (ask my wife), and if the passion & drive isn't there for me, the results will show it. But, I know my strength. I'm a beast (at certain things) when I want to be. When I'm motivated, and when I'm passionate about something, I can't be beaten. I won't stop and I won't quit and I won't go away.

I have been asked "Do you ever sleep?" I don't. I pass out. After I'm finished with passing out, I rise and look to dominate. Some refer to this as "grinding." I look at it as "the hustle." We all have that accelerator pedal or hustle. We may just use it in different spurts and durations for different reasons - that is, if at all.

You have to hustle! What do you have if you have no hustle? Do you get the high score on Candy Crush? Did you binge-watch Season 4 of a show you'll forget about on

Netflix? That's all fine, but if you're looking to have more in life and you find yourself spending the most valuable commodity of time in those areas, you most likely will not be setting your world on fire anytime soon. Lollygagging out, Hustle in. You have it, so use it!

Do you remember that cute little DJ story with the happy ending that Uncle Marc just told you? That was head and heart getting on the same page mixed with passion and served in a big, fat bowl of hustle.

Do you know how to become a cage fighter? It's not by reading a book, it's by getting in the freakin' cage! That's how I learned to be a DJ, by DJing. I showed up. I screwed up. I grew up. I hustled.

When you do hustle, when you do start grinding, sticking, moving - do you know what happens? You create momentum. The "Big Mo." Momentum is hard to create, and when you have it, you need to keep that bad boy rolling. If you pay attention, hustle creates momentum. Momentum fosters opportunities. Enough opportunities will father success. Not luck. Success.

In the "Playing To Win" Chapter of this book, I discussed how my own personal journey actually came to fruition with the hustle. Hustle did create momentum, which created opportunity, which equated to success. There was no luck, and I don't believe in it. Following that passion of mine for music allowed me to become a

DJ, which opened doors for professional wrestling, which grew my network and connected me with owners of an arena football team where I not only became a co-owner, but was in charge of game day operations and performed music in the stadium during games. The performing, the showmanship, the confidence all granted me the courage and opportunity to become a lead vocalist for a Christian Rock Band. It was amazing! Did I get lucky again and again, or did I hustle?

Most strong, successful people didn't have an easy past. They had obstacles and issues just as much if not more than everyone else. The difference is they followed their heart, fought on and hustled their tails off. That's what gets it done.

Unless your religious beliefs are one that prohibits you from the use of having electricity, then you should know the name Ryan Seacrest. This multimillionaire's professional career of spinning gigs like plates has him involved in projects from TV hosting to radio hosting to TV producing to film to philanthropy and the list goes on. Managing editor of E! News, New Year's Eve Ball dropping, Top 40 radio countdowns, American Idol hosting, radio personality of KIIS-FM, television co-host of Live With Kelly And Ryan, and producing shows which spin off other celebs such as the Kardashians, are just a few of the projects in which the "King" has been involved.

Known as the "busiest man in showbiz," Seacrest has had his own thoughts on hustling and how it's created the career he has desired and earned. He's been quoted as saying "Mine's a pretty simple strategy: There's not a lot of talent here, but there's a lot of hustle. I have to be in every place I can and be busy." He's also gone on the record with "I knew I could control one thing, and that is my time and my hours and my effort and my efficiency." He doesn't get lucky. He hustles.

"Oh yeah" you may think to yourself, "but he's Ryan Seacrest." Well, sure. *Now* he's Ryan Seacrest. Did they look at him the same when he was the short, no talent, chubby kid growing up in Georgia? Or did it march more to the beat of something like "And the award for 'Most Likely Getting Picked Last In Gym Class' goes to…Ryan Seacrest." Yawn. The dude hustled to get to wherever he wanted to go and still does! It's a mindset and a lifestyle.

Jerry Rice is considered by many as the greatest professional football player of all time. The three time Super Bowl Champion, Hall Of Fame wide receiver not only owns records for the most receptions and most touchdowns in NFL History, but the incredible - and seemingly untouchable - record of 22,895 career receiving yards. "Untouchable?" Really? Aren't records made to be broken? There isn't a current active player that is within even 10,000 yards of touching that! In order for that to be broken, someone would need a career of two *healthy* decades of 1,000-yard seasons. Every year.

So, yeah. Jerry is the greatest. He probably wasn't lucky, but he sure must have been talented, right? Of course he was, you ding-dong, but so are hundreds of the other greatest players who literally do not come close to him. So what set this Superman apart from the pack? The hustle.

Rice's work ethic was a thing of legend. His training schedule was rigorous on light days. I've heard stories of teammates watching him run routes while they came to the Stadium looking to pickup checks *after* they've already won the Super Bowl. Routes. Off-season!

Factually speaking, he was quite legendary for his off-season workouts alone. They were usually six-day-a-week workouts where the afternoons were dedicated to weights and strength training. The mornings were the key and focused more on the cardiovascular aspect. Rice had a daily five-mile run which was all uphill on a mountain. At the steepest part of the trail, he would run ten 40-meter wind sprints. Ten! Uphill! If I do one forty meter sprint on flat ground you can call the funeral home to make arrangements. How was this documented? There were witnesses. Other NFL greats of the day would join Rice from time to time to train with him. They were always invited and they mostly all got sick before the end of the day because of the brutality of the workout. Ever see Jerry Rice winded? Neither did defenses. Hustle.

IN THE END

"Everything will be okay in the end.
If it's not okay, it's not the end."

- John Lennon

Back to my friend - the one who lost his job? Well, he actually never "lost" it, they just *took* it from him, but I digress. Anyhow, he never answered my text that morning. I also called and left a voicemail. Nothing. I stalked him on Facebook (you all know you do it), and no updates. I was starting to get a little concerned.

I reached out again the next day and he answered to the tune of "No big deal, bro." He was very lucid, very reflective and for me, surprisingly calm.

Hold on. He just had his career, his livelihood ripped away and he's calm? Very. His approach to his circumstance was the catalyst for me to pull this particular chapter together. This was absolutely an instance where head, heart and hustle were on the same page.

With his head he had clear perspective. He explained to me that this j-o-b (just over broke) that he's been going to for years has been increasingly stifling. Not only was it not benefiting him great financial gains, it wasn't fulfilling him. He's a people person, a leader and has a desire to interact with others, not send emails, sit at a desk and say "Yes, sir." He realized that if he never lost his position with the company in the first place, then he would have never been uncomfortable enough to have to make a move. He probably would have stayed in the mundane, not living life until retirement. Who likes that? Nobody.

Although there is the anxiety of uncertainty, his heart soared with the opportunity of possibilities. He realized now the reset button had been activated and he had been given a chance. He can start over and try to do it his way. Coaching. Teaching. Kids. Being active. Being involved with community. That's where his heart desires to be. That's the direction he wants to go.

His hustle was clear. He has connections. He's already been involved in some networks where doors could be opened once he starts to knock. If not, he would knock harder. His wife teaches and has networks. There are openings. There are possibilities. He was going to firm up and update certifications and then get at it. He was going to hustle.

The only thing this was the end of, was a chapter in his life he was happy to be done with. It wasn't the end, it was clearly just the beginning.

———

HUNGRY

Have you ever been hungry? No. I mean really, really hungry?

Have you ever been in that place - that spot - where you have had laser vision and wanted that one thing so bad that you would do anything, almost anything to get it?

In the late 1990s I was a mailman. I remember one particular day being in the hills of Pennsylvania on an all driving route, pulling over in my truck for a quick stretch break. This was about the time I would run into that dude who delivered newspapers on the same day, at the same time, once a week. Yeah, this brother was a little bit crazy, but I liked him, and he was definitely passionate.

One particular day we spoke the universal language. No, we didn't speak about love, we spoke about money. I didn't have any, and he had less. He told me he had *tears burning down his cheeks in the shower* that morning, praying that he would find a way out and he would do whatever it took (without harming anyone) to make it happen. Whatever it took. He was hungry. So hungry. I wish I could've help him, but my own rib cage was starting to show, too. He wasn't asking for help, but even if he was - what could I do? I was tight. That would be as if trying to save someone from drowning when you can't swim.

We are trained wrong. There is a stigma that "rich is bad" and "you get what you get, and don't get upset." Really? That's garbage. How can you help yourself, your family, your friends, your community, or your charity if you are consumed with keeping your own head above water? You can't.

Get hungry. Get Big. Real big. Start asking questions. Put yourself out there to serve. Get uncomfortable already! It's so not about you. Network your face off and do what you have to as if you had your *tears burning down your cheeks in the shower.*

No. Do what you have to do as if your son, daughter, baby, grandparent or someone you love had THEIR *tears burning down their cheeks in the shower.*

Dammit. You, I, and all of us can do more. We need to do more. Let's stop being lazy. Let's stop being comfy. Let's stop being scared. Let's get out of our own head and out of our own way. Let's start a revolution of inspiration. Let's get at it! Get hungry, stay hungry and start hunting.

COMFORT ZONE

*"A ship in harbor is safe, but that is not what
ships are built for."*

\- John A. Shedd

The sign should read "Welcome to The Comfort Zone -
the most dangerous place on Earth." Neon hazard signs
should be blinking everywhere at the entrance gates.

The comfort zone is dangerous. *Your* comfort zone is
dangerous.

"My comfort zone" you're thinking? "But it's comfortable!"

Yes. Yours. First, I tell you that your excuses suck, and
now I'm telling you that your cozy, convenient spot is
treacherous. I know what you're thinking too. You're
thinking "Shoot the messenger."

Am I writing this book to serve you some warm milk
and cookies, administer bellywubs and tuck you into your
blanky? C'mon now. I'm bringing this to you as I'd want

someone to break it down to me. I'm not looking to kill trees, waste ink, waste time, and especially not waste my time. I'm busy. There's laundry to do. Is that obnoxious? Got your attention? Good.

So back to this comfort zone thing. I remember when I stepped out of my comfort zone and stepped into network marketing. All network marketing is, is simply marketing a product or service to your network of family and friends. By cutting out the middle man, you get paid for referrals. You can send 50 friends to your favorite restaurant and you won't be offered a free appetizer. In network marketing, you can refer those same 50 friends and get paaaaid for those referrals. Big time, too. Sounds like a sweet deal, right? Sure. Now it does. Today, its mainstream and there is a multitude of info everywhere about the industry. Forbes Magazine has talked about it, major universities have courses on it, and even brand named companies are pulling their products off of shelves to lend their business model to the sleek, savvy format of network marketing. When I started, I didn't have a clue as to what I was doing, or how it worked.

Despite myself, somehow I quickly promoted to the first level of management in the company as a district manager. This was basically my first pay raise with the company. I still hadn't mastered this new journey, but I was party-rocking and popping corks off champagne bottles all the way to the bank, baby! Woot - Woot! High five? Anyone?

Anyhow, after taking a break from signing autographs, shaking hands and kissing babies, I accompanied my wife, who already was an executive national vice president in our company, to a local but rather large company event. Attending this event was then company President Rita Davenport. Rita was and still is incredible. Keynote motivational speaker, acclaimed author and television personality are just a few of her credentials, none of which surpass the fact that she is one of the most caring, authentic people you will ever meet. She's also a straight shooter, and she had some pearls of wisdom for me.

"Congratulations on your promotion to district manager," she said as her smile faded and my wife's had gotten bigger. "It's a great place to get to, you just don't want to stay there too long. Now let's take a selfie."

Ouch. Right. Back to reality. I haven't quite reached the mountaintop, yet. More work to do. Thank you for the gentle reminder, Rita.

So why is the comfort zone such a terrible place to reside? Good is not only the enemy of bad, it is the enemy of great. You heard it here first, or maybe not. Regardless, good is the enemy of great. Comfortable sets you up for failure. Comfortable is dangerous. Any good CEO, coach, manager, boss, owner, zookeeper, whatever…knows this. Any great one, will keep you from going there.

A business exceeds market projections and has a fabulous quarter. After a quick company boosting reward or even get together, there's a new goal with (hopefully) an incentive attached. The CEO creates a "back to work" environment with focus. If the CEO doesn't create a "back to work" environment, there may not be work to get back to. They can't get lazy.

A sports team crushes an opponent over the weekend. Monday the coach (if the coach is experienced) will come onto the field, court, rink, etc, and probably won't be in too stellar of a mood. The coach isn't looking to have an airport named after him just yet. If he rests on the laurels of last weekend, guess how next weekend could turn out?

What sense does all this make? The company crushed it! The team dominated! Shouldn't they be able to chest bump and take a break? What happened to "celebrating the small victories along the way?" Isn't that still a "thing?" Sure it is, for about a minute. They can't get too comfortable. Well, actually they can get comfy, but if while being complacent they aren't expecting a letdown for the next challenge, they're not only comfortable, they're foolish too.

If the employees are too busy breaking their arms while patting themselves on the back, and the team is late getting onto the field because they are more worried about chilling the champagne for the post-game party, you will usually see a sign. I'm not talking about a sign from above, I'm talking about a blinking, glowing neon one that screams "Failure Straight Ahead."

UPSET

"Destroy what destroys you."

- Unknown

We all know the term "Upset." I don't mean your ice cream melted or the dog peed on the carpet kind of upset, I mean the David and Goliath kind of upset. Both are tough scenarios. It's a hard pill to swallow. It's a fairytale victory for the person, player, candidate or team who plays "Cinderella," but for the powerhouse "could have" or "should have" been victor it's just demoralizing.

If that coach, who's team just skull thumped their opponent 35-0 on Saturday, doesn't come in with a crabby, sobering "You better get ready for this week's opponent" attitude on Monday, he's asking for defeat. If that CEO doesn't take the momentum from the incredible last quarter and set a higher goal, it's going to be a dismal payday for many.

Do you remember the greatest movie from 1982? Rocky III? Sure you do! This featured Hulk Hogan as "Thunderlips," Mr. T as the nasty villain "Clubber Lang," and featured the hit song "Eye Of The Tiger" by Survivor. That's some good pop culture right there, people. Everyone loves that movie!

Well, everyone except my Canadian friend Samantha McLeod. Sammi visited Philadelphia back in 2016, and my wife Christina and I met her for a marvelous dinner. Before we got her to her final destination in Pennsylvania - the Philly Airport, we gave her a quick tour of the city. I explained how iconic the steps of the Philadelphia Art Museum are - not because of the art, of course - but because of the city's fictional Super Hero "Rocky" who ran up them!

She looked at me just like my wife usually looks at me, as if she had no clue on the planet as to what I was talking about. She thought I was joking. I thought *she* was joking. Really? Rocky? Who hasn't heard of Rocky? Apparently, Canadians.

"Wait, are you serious?" I asked

"Leave her alone," Christina chimed in.

"Leave her alone? I'm helping her!" I was perplexed, Christina was mortified and Samantha was unfazed. Next, you would think we couldn't take her for Philly Cheese Steaks because she was vegan or something. Wait, that happened too. Busting her chops? Of course I am, but it's only because we love our Sammi.

Anyhow, back to Rocky III. Yes, friends. Clearly, I know this is just a movie, but it's the principle of the movie. For my underprivileged friends like Samantha and everyone in the entire country of Canada, allow me to give you a quick synopsis.

Rocky was a laughable underdog in the first two movies until he upsets the Muhammad Ali like Champion "Apollo Creed" at the end of Rocky II through obsessive determination and hard work. Rocky III showcases Sylvester Stallone (Rocky) as the now polished Champion who is more concerned about posing for pictures and how his hair looks in his latest credit card commercial rather than focusing on staying hungry.

Mr. T (Clubber Lang) is nasty. He's an unknown to many but a powerful, aggressive challenger seeking fame, fortune and glory through a title shot, literally breaking guys in half trying to get it.

Spoiler alert. They finally meet and Challenger embarrassingly destroys Champion. In the end Rocky obviously wins it back. How else could they have shot the other 37 Rocky movies if he didn't?

Point being, this amazing Champ got upset. The difference? The Champ got into a comfort zone. He achieved the big house, fancy cars and all the popularity. The Challenger was sweating, grinding, killing himself in disgusting, dank basements training like a beast. He was so not comfortable. He had the "Eye Of The Tiger" (I couldn't resist). It was only until Rocky got himself back into that carnivorous, psychotic place of determination where he could rise to defeat his enemy.

Dramatic? Sure, it's Hollywood - and in the '80s, baby! But don't discount the message. That comfort zone will leave you in a soft, vulnerable state. The old saying is "The comfort zone is a beautiful place, but nothing ever grows there." Noted. I just believe it is deeper than that. It's downright dangerous.

AMBITION

"There goes my Hero, watch him as he goes."
- Dave Grohl of the Foo Fighters

Both of my sons wrestle for their schools. One is on the high school team, the other is in the middle school level. This past year, a few of their teammates won the state title in Pennsylvania.

This is how my brain works. When it comes to amateur wrestling, these boys are the best in the state of Pennsylvania. Pennsylvania is one of the best states in the country. America is one of the best countries in the world. Does that mean these boys are the best in the world? Mind blown. The answer is debatable but I do know this. The day after they won their state titles, do you know where they wound up? Practice. Back on the mats. I absolutely love it. They're not comfortable. They're ambitious.

When my daughter was 10 years old, my wife and I took her to a noncompetitive beauty pageant. We thought she would love it (she did), and the rest is history. But "the rest" happened as I'll explain next.

An unannounced visit from a talent scout happened the morning of the show. She set up shop in the lobby and all the girls from all ages absolutely mobbed her. After the single line of hopeful, would be stars was formed, and order was restored, directions were clear. Walk up to the talent scout. Take a photo. Say your name and what your special "talent" is. Leave. They'll call you.

The process went something like this.

"My name is Ashley. I sing and dance." Next.

"I am Veronica. I sing and dance." Next.

"Hello. I'm Madison and I sing and dance." Next up was my daughter.

"Hi! My name is Jayda, and I like to speak publicly."

That was it. Off we were, and it got crazy. Back and forth for auditions from where we lived in Pennsylvania to New York City was an all day affair, and it was frequent. We attended auditions, and what they call "go sees" and went for anything and everything for which she could be potentially cast. I believe when she was cast

on her first part, they were looking for an Asian girl. So
not Asian. Nailed it!

On one ofs the first major auditions she attended, she
had friends there. On the way home J expressed how
upset she was that she had to "compete" against her
friends. I explained to her that you cheer for each other,
you support each other, but you go for yours. Sometimes
you'll get it, sometimes they'll get it. There's enough sun-
shine for everyone to get a tan. I also explained this is
the nature of the business, and if she didn't like it, then
we shouldn't do the business. She got it.

Since then, Jayda has appeared on live television for
QVC, walked runways for New York City and Philadelphia Fashion Week, has been in countless newspapers
and magazines, and has appeared in commercials that
have aired internationally on Disney, Nickelodeon, and
A&E. She didn't get comfortable and she's still not.

My oldest son Kane? He literally is a musical prodigy.
I play other people's music really well, but that's about
where it stops with me, so I'm not sure from where he
gets it. The kid rocks drums, bass, lead, rhythm, electric
and acoustic guitar. He plays piano and writes tons of his
own music for himself and the bands in which he per-
forms. He recorded the theme music for my show laying
four video tracks in less than 45 minutes.

The young man is very gifted and always has been since he literally was an infant. He can show up to places, sit in, play by ear and just perform. He is the prime candidate to be comfortable. Besides all the other things 16-year-olds his age seem to have interest in (money, girls, etc), do you know how he spends his spare time? He's writing music. Recording new tracks. Writing new jams. Driving me crazy driving him all over the place to get music lessons. Did you read what I just wrote about this kid? Yes, he still takes music lessons. He probably doesn't need to at this point, but he does it because he's looking to grow and not get comfortable. He found his passion and has ambition.

Am I a proud father bragging about my kids? Definitely. Are they worthy to brag about in this example? 100 percent. Stay with me and let's roll with this.

Kane and I attend concerts whenever someone comes around that at least one of us wants to see. Together the father and son, DJ and musician combo, have seen tons of acts ranging from some of the biggest icons to some of the most undercover of the underground.

Kane's favorite band is the Foo Fighters. You may not need to be a fan of theirs, or even a fan of music to know that the lead vocalist is the legendary Dave Grohl. The now-frontman for more than 20 years was previously known as being the drummer for that little trio band from Seattle known simply as…Nirvana. You know, the ones who killed off '80s hair band music and ushered in an era of grunge? Yep. Them.

Grohl is a man of many hats. He not only runs the Foo, but he is also known for performing in other bands as well. Over the years, he has rocked in Queens Of The Stone Age, Probot, the supergroup Sound City Players and Them Crooked Vultures who was a mix of Queens Of The Stone Age, Nirvana and Led Zeppelin.

The list of who he has collaborated with is unprecedented. Can we just leave it at everyone? Puff Daddy, Paul McCartney, Stevie Knicks, LL Cool J, Led Zeppelin, Prince, David Bowie, Tom Petty and the Heartbreakers, Nine Inch Nails, Joan Jett, The Zach Brown Band, The Bangles, Pearl Jam, Queen, Lemmy Kilmister from Motorhead and Slash from Guns 'N Roses are all part of and just some of the the Dave Grohl Club.

In the summer of 2015, Grohl was performing a world tour with the Foo Fighters. One night in Gothenburg, Sweden, he fell off the stage causing immediate emergency personnel to rush to the injured lead vocalist. Immediately, he was taken backstage for medical attention. The band is so talented that Foo Drummer Taylor Hawkins continued lead vocals as the show always does, and must go on.

News spread that Grohl had a severe leg break. However, after a few songs were performed, he reappeared ON A STRETCHER with an assistant who "held his leg in place" as he sang and played guitar on three songs! Is this even real? You betcha. Go check Youtube. As he came BACK out later he addressed the crowd saying "I've been to a lot of Foo Fighter shows, but I've never been to one like this." Neither had anyone else! The band played on throughout the night to the massive crowd for most of the show (obviously without their leader), covering songs from Queen, The Rolling Stones, Van Halen and Alice Cooper. Good thing the Foo Fighters are, as Dave Grohl puts it, "The Most Expensive Cover Band In The World."

Fourth of July 2015 there I was with Kane in Washington DC, at RFK Stadium for the Foo Fighters 20th Anniversary Blowout Concert. Heart, Joan Jett and The Blackhearts, LL Cool J and even the legendary Buddy Guy were part of the festival. The buzz and concern days leading up to it was if Dave Grohl was going to be able to perform because of health issues regarding the grueling injury to his leg.

He did. On a throne. Not just any throne. It was a custom made Dave Grohl Throne that lit up and moved all about the stage. King Arthur would have been jealous. The place was nuts for their 90-minute set as Grohl sat with his cast, his guitar and incited a riot-like atmosphere to the obliging crowd. The night ended with fireworks as my exhausted son and I realized we just participated in a piece of the all time great music puzzle.

So, based on everything that I just told you about my son's favorite band, does Dave Grohl have ambition? Does he sound comfortable to you? This iconic, multi-millionaire rockstar doesn't need to do anything - anything - else with his life, but he keeps pushing.

Nirvana is already in the Rock And Roll Hall Of Fame. Expect the Foo Fighters to join them at some point. Don't be surprised if Dave Grohl someday gets in for his solo efforts of collaborating with the all time greats. That would be a true triple play hat trick, and it has never been done before.

Maybe it will happen, maybe it won't happen. But this conversation would never have happened if Dave Grohl lived in his comfort zone. Get uncomfortable.

RANT #8

PERSPECTIVE

I don't want to say it's the most important thing, but it ranks pretty high; like oxygen.

I saw a comedian on late-night TV speaking about how we are all so spoiled. He was using the example of airlines and how as people we love to complain. He mentioned how we tend to get bent out of shape if the chair doesn't go back far enough or if the wifi doesn't work. "You have to remember, you sit in a chair. It flies in the sky, for hundreds of miles an hour! New York to L.A. takes five hours. It use to take 30 years! People would die along the way, babies would be born…you would arrive with a whole 'nother group of people!"

Funny? Yes. True? Yes. Gratitude and appreciation are a big part of perspective.

A few years back, I was asked to speak to a high school football team. The players had become somewhat blase over a few seasons going from state champions to a 1-9 squad the year before. I wanted to give them perspective and a little inspiration, starting with their head coach. I told them the story of their hometown Coach Barry Blauvelt.

When he played Pop Warner Football, he was the kid who wasn't necessarily that athletic. Frankly speaking, he was slow, chubby and was easy to knock around, but Barry wasn't afraid to work, and you can't measure heart. Fortunately for him, he had a ton of it.

As the years passed and his dedication grew, so did his diet, his time in the weight room, and his journey as a student of the game who loved watching game film. He became the starting left tackle (or "blind side" as so many refer to the position today) for the Varsity team. That year the Wallington Panthers won the State Championship. Barry was a State Champion.

Where most stories would end, this story just begins. Number 75 went off to college and played. At the end of his college career, he returned to his hometown to fulfill his passion of the game as a coach. Eventually he became head coach, and led his team to the Playoffs. Playoffs led to the Championship. The Championship was played at Giants Stadium. Actually, the then brand new Met Life Stadium. Yes, the Met Life Stadium where the New York Football Giants played. When the game was said and done, New Jersey's own Wallington Panthers became state

Champions in the Meadowlands. Fact - Barry Blauvelt coached the first team to ever officially win a championship in Met Life Stadium. Whoah! As he hoisted the trophy up for all to see, Barry was carried off the field by his players. Barry was a State Champion Coach for the very organization he played as a kid.

State Champion Player. State Champion Coach. Boyhood dreams came true. Hometown Hero. The night I had the opportunity to speak to his new team, I dropped perspective in that locker room. You don't "have" to play for Coach Barry, you "get" to play for Coach Barry. The night ended with all players tearing up voluntary wind sprints in the rain. This was after they already practiced. Perspective is powerful.

My friend Desire was somewhat apprehensive about going for her doctorate. She already had her Masters Degree and had been a teacher for years but couldn't completely envision the bigger picture for herself. After we connected on a 15-minute phone call, she caught my vision and perspective.

The question wasn't why *should* she go for her doctorate, the question was actually why *shouldn't* she go for her doctorate. She just didn't have that perspective. Toward the end of our call, once she stepped back and saw things with a broader scope, she was telling me why she was definitely going to go for it. I'm proud of her.

Perspective is huge. In traffic? You have a car. Your meal isn't just the way you like it? You get to eat. Your golf game stunk today? Please, don't even go there. Become half-full and get some appreciative, grateful perspective.

8

DREAMS

"The person who takes no chances generally has to take whatever is left when others are through choosing."

\- Napoleon Hill

Remember when you were a kid and anything was possible? The future was wide open. The world was a clean slate. You had dreams, baby! Many of us knew what we wanted to be when we grew up.

I loved professional wrestling. Oooh yeah! I had posters of every single guy taped on every single inch of the paneled walls of my room. While most girls my age had posters of Rick Springfield or Duran Duran on their bedroom doors, I had Sgt. Slaughter and Andre The Giant. Bloody men dressed in tights hitting each other with chairs and barbwire was how I rolled.

I remember it clearly. I was in first grade and the teacher asked the class to draw a picture of what we were going to be when we grew up. Oh man, I created this masterpiece! All along the outline of the page were the bad guy heel wrestlers. The giant in black trunks with that 1970s style afro, the guy dressed as a bird with the mask of an eagle, and a caveman waving a club were all there just to name a few.

In the center of the page there I was in all my glory. Literally. I was wearing blue wrestling trunks and had my feathered blonde hair (my hair was brown) and a crimson mask of blood dripping down my fan favorite, baby-face forehead. I had that gold-plated, World Championship belt strapped across my six-pack waist. This, of course, was when I actually had hair and abs, but back to the picture.

Both of my cannon-like arms are being raised in victory by this little, bald referee. I actually drew the ref too small so as he's holding my arms up, he's dangling from the ground making me look even more massive than I planned. I can't possibly imagine what Mrs. Slominski thought as she reviewed the completed assignments that night. Fireman, doctor, librarian…cage fighter. Great.

Crazy? Unrealistic? Maybe. But I had dreams. Many of us did. Let me ask you a question. What happened?

Seriously. What happened? Where did our childhood dreams go? Did we lose interest? Did we lose faith? Did someone - did the world tell you it was crazy? It was unrealistic? Stupid? Were you made to believe that you weren't good enough?

In 2015, I was cleaning out my home and purging as we were in the beginning stages of a potential move. I was finding all kinds of crazy things that have followed me over time. A certificate? Oh, right. I was in the Cub Scouts. Anyhow, I came across several - tons actually - of completed homework assignments, art projects, and various schoolwork from all my children from over the years.

I came across one particular assignment from one of my children completed in what looks to be the first few days of second grade. Now, I will not reveal this child's birth name in efforts to protect the rights of the inno-cent. As a matter of fact, we will change this child's name temporarily for the sake of this chapter. Let's go with a gender neutral friendly name. Let's go with…"Pat."

Now, I believe this specific assignment was similar to the one I had when I was a child, and it seems as if the class was instructed to list what their long term and short term life goals were.

There were six bullet points that my child listed. "Pat" titled his paper "Dreams." I would like to share this unknowing masterpiece. Keep in mind what you are about to read is a list that comes from an untarnished, crazy, beautiful, genius and belief driven 7-year-old-mind. Together, let us review Pat's Dreams.

#1 TO BE "AWSOME"

Great advice! Who doesn't want to be awesome? Have you ever seen that image on social media that reads "Don't forget to be awesome?" Well, don't! Go out and be awesome, because you are. Are you rolling your eyes? Yeah? Well, let's be clear. That's not on me, that's on you. Adjust your thinking to adjust your results. Stop being a hater and start being awesome. You have too much to offer and need to break that limited mindset.

Please, for the sake of this planet, get out into the world and go share your awesomeness wherever you may roam. While you're at it, go sprinkle and plant some awesome seeds along the way. Help others be awesome, too. That will make you even more awesome.

What's stopping you? Is it a lack of self-belief just like "poor lady" in the chapter titled "Special." She was special, she just never realized it. Is it that others will mock your efforts or refreshed attitude? Is that stopping you? No worries. You're in good company. Flip back to the "Success & What We Tell Ourselves" Chapter. Thank goodness Steve Jobs, Oprah, Walt Disney, Michael Jordan or The Beatles didn't listen to people's fleeting, fickled opinions. What a boring place this would be. I'm so glad they chose to go against the grain and made a DECISION to be awesome. You should too.

In this particular list, Pat ranks it first - as it should be. The only constructive criticism and advice I would offer the lad at this point would be to spell it correctly. The first step in being awesome is actually spelling the word "awesome" right. But give the kid a break. As my editor Cathy and grammar teachers across the globe squirm, remember he was seven! I digress. Back to you. Go be awesome. Throw that stuff around!

#2 NO HOMEWORK FOR ME & MY FRIENDS

Alright. Definitely a short term goal. What can I say? Pat is an advocate. He's looking out for himself - and his homies. Very nobel. Very loyal. He's not just saying "Get me out of this heat," but "get my friends out, too." Thanks, Pat. But as Great-Grandma Hayford would say, "Be careful for what you ask for, you just might get it."

This reminds me of the scene from that Bill Murray movie "Stripes."

Sergeant Hulka: "We got a full day ahead of us. We're gonna start out with a five mile run." (Soldiers groan)

Bill Murray: "I know that I'm speaking for the entire platoon when I say this run should be postponed until this platoon is better rested."

Sergeant Hulka: "We'll, I'll tell you what, soldier. Let's make it 10 miles."

Unfortunately, things don't always work out as planned.

You know, after reassessing number 2 on the list, I've come to a conclusion. If this gets pushed through, there are gonna be some pretty dumb kids running around. But hey, this Pat kid has his heart in the right place, and that's important. It's imperative to be an advocate for others. The sick, the weak, the poor, the needy, the voiceless all need help. You can't save the world by yourself, but you can save many and start a good kind of revolution by having a good heart and caring for others.

Have a heart. Care for others. Be an advocate. Why don't we rename number 2 from being "No Homework For Me & My Friends" to "Care For Others."

#3 TO BE A SUPERHERO

How cool is this? Don't even act like you wouldn't want to be a Superhero! Think of some of the Superheroes out there today.

Take Spiderman. He crawls up walls. He slings webs like hashtags, and the dude has senses beyond any human capabilities.

Wonder Woman? Come on, now. She's badder than Beyonce'! This lady has speed, strength and intelligence unlike anyone else. Her poor husband.

That brings me to Superman. He can do it all. He's the man of steel. He has x-ray vision. He flies. His name is in the title of this category. I mean, he's super!

Let me ask you something. Forget the super kind of heroes. Do we have *any* kind of heroes at all out there these days? Where have the Abraham Lincolns, John F. Kennedys and John Waynes of the world all gone? Are there any more heroes? Anyone? Anywhere?

Of course there are. The difference is they aren't wearing capes and meeting on the golf course together at the Hall Of Justice. They are right in front of our face every single day, and somehow we seem to miss them. They're wearing scrubs in hospitals. They're sitting behind the wheel of that big yellow bus driving our children to and from school. They wear a badge on their chest like a target as they take to the streets every single day. They sit behind a desk and try to motivate 30 different kids at a time in a classroom. They drive an ambulance. They get deployed overseas. They run into burning buildings that are collapsing and are on fire, risking their own lives for people they don't even know. Amazing.

Let me ask you something else. If you were a superhero with a super power, what power would you have? Would you fly? Would you be able to read minds? Would you want to have insurmountable strength?

Whatever that power is, would it be "special?" Would it carry a special energy? Would your power be one of a kind and unique - like a special knack, talent or gift? Maybe like the one of a kind, special knack, talent, gift or energy you bring to the table right now? Think about it.

Hmm. Maybe Pat was onto something. I think we leave the title of number 3 alone.

#4 TO BE SMARTEST IN MY CLASS

Now, I am all about being positive, pulling from deep inside yourself and never giving up. But let me bust out some harsh reality here. Pat will never, and I mean never ever achieve his number 4 goal of being "Smartest In My Class" if Pat decides to roll with his actual number 2 idea of "No Homework For Me and My Friends."

I think the undertone of this has to be hard work. See, you can be good. You can be real good on your own skill all day long, but to be great is something else. That takes hard work. Consistent work. Working and toiling while they party and play. Dedication equals results, and results equals respect.

Again, all day long hard work beats talent when talent doesn't work hard. Think about it. You can be good at something, but while you're taking a break, taking a short cut, worrying about how you look doing it, there is someone out there who is hungry. They are taking one more step. They take one less break. They are doing one more thing. They'll do whatever it takes. That my friend, is ultimately who is going to win. Hard work does beat talent when talent doesn't work hard.

Pat should know. As a fifth, sixth and seventh grader he would do laps after football practice when all the other kids were playing around and leaving. Harrison…um, Pat became the starting running back and linebacker. Then he became team kicker. How? By taking weekdays of his summer and working - and I do mean working - and training with Massimo Biscardi, who was one of the top 10 high school kickers in the country. Touchdowns, tackles and now 30 yard field goals could be made by this twelve-year-old! Regardless of offense, defense or special teams there were times when he hardly left the game. Remember this - the wolf on top of the hill is not as hungry as the wolf climbing up the hill. Keep climbing up the hill.

Let's give Pat a little direction with number 4 so he can not only be the "Smartest In His Class" but can reach the goal of "Being The Best" in whatever he chooses to do. Let's change the title of "Being The Smartest In My Class" to "Outwork Everyone."

#5 "TO BECOME A PROFESSIONAL GOOD FOOTBALL PLAYER"

There are literally millions of boys and girls who want to and currently do play football. Many of these children dream of growing up like the athletes we see on television today, and want to become professionals.

Pay close attention to number 5's Title. The key word here is "good." It sets the overall tone. Notice this isn't listed as "To Become A Professional 'Bad' Football Player," because unfortunately Lord knows we've seen enough of them. Now, knowing Pat, I'm sure the intention of the word "good" has nothing to do with Hero or Villain. Pat meant success.

I however would like to gently rework this Title from "To Become A Professional Good Football Player" to "Role Model." Are you a role model? Sure you are. Is there someone who looks up to you, watches or notices how you walk, talk, serve? No? Nobody on your social media pays attention? At all?

We all are. The decision just needs to be made if you will be a good one, or a bad one. For the record, you don't need to be on TV, trending worldwide or on some electronic billboard. Sure, it helps. By the way, if you are looking to reach more people that way, please refer back to number 4. Outwork everyone.

We are all role models. Good or bad, you are an advocate for yourself. Your family, your friends, the people in your community are all affected by your energy. Remember that energy I mentioned earlier? Well, yeah. That. You have it. What are you going to do with it? How will you use it? Here's an idea - be a "Professional Good Football Player," or better yet - "Be A Role Model."

#6 TO BE A TREE

And that brings us to this. So profound, so philosophical was everything up to this point. And now, the kid wants to be a tree. I mean, it is what it is. I wanted to be David Lee Roth at one point, so maybe this was just a phase. Maybe he was pulling the teacher's leg. Maybe he was being rebellious. Pat has a fantastic imagination so I'm not looking too deep into this one. Pat wanted to be a tree.

Or not. I'm gonna go on a limb here (insert laughter), but take a step back for a moment and bear with me.

Where I live now is a tremendous contrast from where I was raised. The little boy who grew up on Locust Avenue (yes, the street that was named after a bug) in North Jersey didn't have a garden, front yard or flower bed. Today, my family and I reside on a quiet cul-de-sac in Pennsylvania where the scenery very much resembles that of a forest. One day as I was driving down my street, I stopped for a moment just to take it all in. Hundreds and hundreds of trees surround everyone's homes. They go as deep as the eye can see and align the horizon. I envisioned what the landscape would look like if they were all gone. It wouldn't just be barren, it would look stupid. Something wouldn't be right without all of those magnificent trees.

Think of how critical trees are to our everyday life. The book you are holding, maybe the couch or chair you are sitting on, and the building you are inside of may all be created from trees. Maybe you are reading this outdoors in the shade which is provided by, that's right, a tree.

They provide shelter. They protect. They give life. They bear fruit and feed. Trees create oxygen. Trees decorate our land. They offer safety and homes to animals. Some trees are majestic and towering. Some offer privacy to people's property and homes. Some create vibes of calm near a beach or ocean. Sometimes they warn us of harsh weather when wind whips through them, or seduce us into relaxation by responding to a light breeze. They offer happiness for children when they hide behind, or climb up them. They tell us what seasons are coming and going with the arrival, departure, or changing colors of their leaves. They can be guarding with that quiet, superior strength they possess when they are packed together. Trees are completely taken for granted, offer everything in the world that is good, and are absolutely and utterly extraordinary.

Pat is genius. He gets it from his mother. After further consideration, we aren't even coming close to adjusting number 6. How dare I even consider touching it. Trees are righteous, serving and constantly benefitting anyone who is around them. Pat wants to be a tree. Hopefully, this was a metaphor, but either way I think more of us could benefit ourselves and others if we too wanted to "Be A Tree."

DREAMS COME TRUE

In review, Pat's list of "Dreams" is pretty intense. The translated life goals are:

1) Be Awesome
2) Care For Others
3) Be Special
4) Outwork Everyone
5) Be A Role Model
6) Be A Tree

Not bad for a 7 year old. Amazing, really. Pat nailed this assignment. In my book he's already hit all six of these goals and hopefully this awesome, caring, special, hard working, role model of a tree continues to do this on a higher level. I'm not sure what grade he was given on this, but in my book it's a first honor success.

Dreams do come true. Let me explain so you don't dismiss me as a feel good, Disney cartoon made for kids. Dreams do come true if you fight for them. If you nurture them. If you take action for them. If you CREATE opportunities for them to come to life. Dreams do come true if you start by visualization.

As for my first grade assignment, that was a success as well. My childhood dream came true. Do you remember the picture I drew of myself with the championship wrestling belt strapped across my waist as the bad guys surrounded me and the little, bald ref with his feet dangling was raising my arm? Well, it actually happened. Sort of.

I became the little, bald ref raising arms. I was able to do it on nationally syndicated programs. Thousands and thousands perform that task all over the world, and I am able to say that I am in the select group that was able to do it at the most elite level in the world.

My "dream" literally became reality. That reality came with a price, and I had to chase it. Injury, ridicule, rejection was all part of the cost, but when you refuse to accept "no," it can happen. Most people don't believe that, because most people won't put the effort, time and sweat into what it takes to - literally - make the dream come true.

Trust me - get a dream. Visualize it. Chase it down and own it. It's never easy, but it's always worth it.

CLOSING RANT

―――――

SCARS

I want you to know that when this whole thing is over, we are going to have scars, but it is all worth it. And it is beautiful. Your scars are not blemishes, accidents or disfigurements.

The countless years of losses, the injuries, the church bringing your family food, losing your family car, being stagnate in your business is all worth it. The humiliations, the doubt, the mistakes, the fear that you fought through, the failures, the times when you were just wrong and you had to admit it, all mean something. All those moments of frustration and tears, the failed relationships and the moments that scared you so bad that made you question everything and gave clarity are over.

Don't hate your scars. Don't be bitter. They shaped us. Those scars are proof of the healing, power and resilience that are you. They don't hurt anymore. Acknowledge and glorify them. Why shouldn't you? You earned them. Appreciate, grow and acknowledge the scars. They are proof of a past, demand respect and scream wisdom. Those scars that helped bring you here and now prove that you are able to take it, grow and draw strength from them.

Love those scars. They tell stories. Your scars are just like you; unique and priceless. Just like how every leaf in those masterful trees are different, the scars you have are the only ones like them in the universe. Show them proudly to give hope to others.

Your story is one of a kind. Your scars are exotic. You are extraordinary. You are ALIVE and magnificent. Thank you for the gift of you. Go make a difference.

ABOUT THE AUTHOR

Marc Hayford is an American author, inspirational speaker, and entrepreneur.

His mission statement is to work with schools, sports teams, businesses, prisons and individuals to create a higher vision of not what is probable, but what is possible.

Hayford has owned and operated his own DJ company for nearly 20 years, is a veteran of the Armed Forces, and a former professional wrestling referee. He is a network marketing professional, former vocalist and has coached and taught children and adults from everything ranging from football to chess to women's softball. This former state champion weightlifter now hosts his weekly internet show "Monday Mornings With Marc Hayford."

Marc is originally from New Jersey and now resides with his family in Pennsylvania. With all of his accomplishments, his self-proclaimed greatest success is being husband to his wife Christina, and father to his three children Kane, Jayda, and Harrison.